The Flowering of Scotland
Grand Slam '90

—

The Flowering of Scotland Grand Slam '90

Compiled by DEREK DOUGLAS

Bill McLaren
Bill McMurtrie
Brian Meek
David Steele

Foreword by DAVID SOLE

MAINSTREAM PUBLISHING

IN CONJUNCTION WITH

THE GLASGOW HERALD

First published in Great Britain 1990 by
MAINSTREAM PUBLISHING COMPANY (EDINBURGH) LTD
7 Albany Street Edinburgh EH1 3UG
in conjunction with the *Glasgow Herald*

ISBN 1 85158 307 6 (cloth)

British Library Cataloguing in Publication Data

Douglas, Derek   *Glasgow Herald*
The flowering of Scotland: Grand Slam '90
1. Scotland. Rugby union football
I. Title   II. *Glasgow Herald*
796.33309411

ISBN 1-85158-307-6

Typeset in 11/13 Garamond in Great Britain
by Beecee Typesetting Services
Printed in Great Britain by Butler and Tanner, Frome, Somerset

Contents

PREFACE

AT FOUR O'CLOCK on the afternoon of Saturday, 17 March 1990, the public address system at Jenners department store on Edinburgh's Princes Street crackled into life. The predominantly female customers thronging Edinburgh's top store on this glorious spring afternoon expected a sales announcement or maybe, in these troubled times, warning of a bomb scare.

But the proclamation, when it came, was more important than that. 'We have the final result from Murrayfield,' said the disembodied voice, 'Scotland 13, England 7.'

A tumultuous, high-pitched cheer swept around the venerable old store. Matronly Edinburgh ladies and their younger counterparts in the boutiques and at the cosmetics counters realised, as had the Scottish nation — including those poor souls not interested in the game of rugby football — just how significant and historic had been this rugby match. And, like the nation, the Jenners ladies gave vent to a feeling of immense satisfaction that the Auld Enemy had been seen off again.

It has been my privilege to compile this, the *Glasgow Herald* record of Scotland's Grand Slam of 1990. It is intended primarily as a celebration and examination of that magnificent achievement but I have permitted myself the indulgence in this preface of a few personal thoughts on Grand Slam Saturday itself. Perhaps they will strike a chord at least with the 50,000 Scots lucky enough to have had tickets for the game and with the millions more who watched on television.

What a day. Those of us who were there will never forget the passion, the commitment, the excitement — particularly of those closing 15 minutes when the Scottish heroes tackled like demons and played themselves into the history books. Specific moments live still in the mind's eye: the Scottish team, with a stern-faced David Sole at their head, marching from the tunnel with steady and chilling gladiatorial tread; the overwhelmingly emotional experience of 50,000 Scots

7

joining together to sing 'Flower of Scotland' — the very thought of it still sends shivers down the spine. If you weren't there you can have no idea how grand it was and how intimidating it must have been for the England players. This was the day we were going to get our own back for 700 years of slights, real and imagined!

From the game itself there were so many instances of courage, skill and daring that it is perhaps invidious to isolate just a few but I can still re-run the choicest moments like a video tape of the mind.

Take One is Finlay Calder's bone-jarring drive which led to the first successful penalty. The big flanker, socks around his ankles, clutched the ball to his chest with both hands and ploughed, full tilt, into a wall of English forwards. Then, milliseconds later, the Scottish pack, spines in line, drove in behind. That was when the English realised they had a game on their hands.

Take Two has Gavin Hastings getting in that magnificent kick ahead before being knocked out of play just in front of the West stand. I can see Tony Stanger and Rory Underwood sprinting for the line with Fin Calder and Mickey Skinner not far behind. The ball bounced beautifully for the Hawick winger Stanger but it was still a difficult finger-tip take. A great try and a sweet, sweet moment.

Take Three is that wonderful, try-saving tackle by Scott Hastings on Underwood. Live, in the flesh, it was difficult to see just what had happened but later, along with the thousands of others who had their wives videotape the match, it was possible to see just how crucial that tackle had been.

Take Four was, for me, the supreme example of the offensive-defence which won the match for the Scots. We had been under so much pressure. The England skipper, Will Carling, has the ball. He has looked a slippery customer. He is making for the line and we hold our breaths in horror and anticipation. But we need not have feared. He is trapped, and trapped well, by the predatory Scots. Immediately the Scottish pack is there en masse and Carling, with whatever forwards the English could muster, is driven back five, ten metres with such a ferocity that we knew, we just knew then and there, that England were never going to win this game.

My Take Five depicts the most poignant moment of the match. David Bishop has just blown for no-side. Murrayfield erupts with a mixture of relief and jubilation and the youngsters (along with a lot not so young) have begun their traditional pitch invasion. There, down on his knees and with his bowed head resting despairingly on his right hand, is the England hooker, Brian Moore. The uncompromisingly competitive Moore is utterly distraught. Losing hadn't been on his agenda. He is spotted by Finlay Calder who moves through the thronging mass and towards the England pack leader. A protective arm is placed around Moore's shoulders. The players exchange a few words and then swop jerseys. They had been team-mates during the Calder-led tour to Australia the previous summer. Despite the intensity of the foregoing 80 minutes, the tourists' camaraderie is rekindled at the moment of Calder's triumph and Moore's despair. After the rest of the players have left the pitch Calder and Moore trudge slowly towards the safe haven of the police cordon at the tunnel mouth. It would have been easy and understandable for Calder to have raced for the dressing-room so that he could savour the moment of victory with his Scottish team-mates. But he didn't, and that kind of moment is what makes rugby, for my money, still the best team game going.

This, then, is the *Glasgow Herald* book of that historic match and that historic season. It was the year we won the Grand Slam, the Five Nations' Championship, the Triple Crown and the Calcutta Cup. It was the year the English, or at least their media, thought that the glittering prizes would be theirs just for the asking. Why, they even suggested they might declare at half-time. Well they ken better noo!

I would like to thank my fellow contributors who were faced with an almost impossible deadline to make the book happen. Particular thanks must go to my old rugby master, Bill McLaren, who put the finishing touches to his illuminating chapter while on a long-haul flight back from the Hong Kong Sevens. Thanks also to Brian Meek who, in his alter ego as a Conservative politician, had a council election to fight. My gratitude is due, too, to that master statistician, the *Herald*'s rugby correspondent, Bill McMurtrie, and my colleague on the *Herald*'s team of 'Saturday Extra' rugby scribes, David Steele.

We should, too, express thanks to the *Herald* top brass, editor, Arnold Kemp and his deputy, Harry Reid, as they are the people who sanctioned and conceived the book. Grand Slam day was made even sweeter for Harry Reid as, 120 miles north of Murrayfield, Aberdeen FC were handing out a 4-1 thrashing to Hearts!

I must thank too, colleagues on the *Herald* picture, news and sports desks, especially picture editor, George Wilkie. The work of the librarians and the systems staff was also appreciated, as was the generous assistance of the Edinburgh editor, Bob Ross.

Finally, and most sincerely, we must all express our heartfelt gratitude to the Scottish team who triumphed against all the odds and in particular to their skipper, David Sole, who so kindly agreed to write the revealing foreword to this book. It sure was a vintage season and Saturday, 17 March, a day of days. Thanks guys.

DEREK DOUGLAS
March 1990

FOREWORD

BY DAVID SOLE

IF SOMEONE HAD SUGGESTED TO ME six months ago that Scotland would win the Grand Slam, Triple Crown and Calcutta Cup on 17 March 1990, I would probably have laughed in disbelief.

Before the season had begun those most astute observers of form, the book-makers, had made us third favourites, behind England and France. And judging by the form the English players had shown on the previous summer's Lions' tour of Australia they fully justified their position. After four championship weekends they had swept aside Ireland, France and Wales by playing some awesome rugby and had scored over 80 points in the process. Needless to say, this had shortened the odds considerably and had left all of those south of Hadrian's Wall believing that England were going to collect their first honours for a decade.

Scotland had started the season, as far back as October, with a game against the touring Fijians. This we won in fairly convincing style and, with a comfortable victory against Romania also under our belts before Christmas, we looked forward to what the New Year might bring in fairly good heart. The international trial in January revealed little new — the only contentious issue being the appearance of one or two senior players in the junior side which was well beaten. However, as it transpired, these players were soon to be reinstated to the senior side for the championship, where their wealth of experience was no small contributory factor to the success that was to follow.

We saw the first weekend of the championship pass from the comfortable surroundings of the Gleneagles Hotel, although the weekend itself was far from relaxing. Fitness tests, skills work and video sessions occupied our time, all supervised by our own coaches and Jim Blair, the fitness adviser to Auckland and the All Blacks. By the time we were to play our first match, against Ireland in Dublin, we found ourselves in the unaccustomed position of being favourites. This is a mantle that Scots teams have not worn well in the past. We were determined, though, that this was not going to be a drawback despite the fact, also, that Ian McGeechan was laid up with flu. We had extremely competent men to fall back on in Jim Telfer, Douglas Morgan and Derrick Grant who, with Ian, were with us throughout the championship.

Ireland had just been beaten by England, had undergone one or two changes in personnel and were playing in front of their home supporters. They had also just played two of the strongest nations in world rugby, England and New Zealand, and although they had been beaten they were more battle-hardened than ourselves. In the end, Scotland stuttered to an unconvincing win made more worrying by our inability to adapt to the refereeing of the lineouts where we were overwhelmed.

A good deal of hard work was needed, especially as our next game was against France. Played in gale-force conditions, we had use of the wind in the first half and only managed to score three points. Luck, however, was to be on our side. After the break, the wind subsided and in a rash moment Alain Carminati was sent off for stamping. This proved to be the turning point of the game. French heads went down, ours came up and we played with renewed vigour for the rest of the match, both in defence and attack.

A trip to Cardiff is never one which fills anyone with confidence, but with a completely 'new look' Welsh side we felt that this might be our best opportunity in a number of years to come away with a win. I have never before heard such a passionate rendering at Cardiff of 'Land of my Fathers'. The whole nation appeared to be brimming with 'hwyl' — as were the 15 Welsh players. However, early scores and some outstanding tackling saw us come away with a win. In all three games we had not played to our full potential. This was extremely frustrating for the players but at least we were unbeaten and all the prizes were still up for grabs.

Thus, for only the third time in history, the championship was to be decided on its final weekend and, for the first time ever, the match was not going to involve France. The media loved it. While Scotland were playing in Wales, England had a blank weekend and, having watched our game, declared that they had learnt nothing new.

From the Sunday onwards all attention was turned to the Grand Slam showdown on 17 March. The Scots made a conscious decision to play it 'low key' and with the aid of the Scottish Press tried to relieve the pressure on the players. Calls from papers south of the Border were directed to the Scottish Rugby Union where permission would be sought for official clearance. This could be denied if need be. This left the Scottish players free to concentrate on the job in hand and, by the time we came together on the Wednesday night, we were all straining at the leash, already hungry to get to grips with the English.

In England, meanwhile, it appeared that all the talk was of comparisons with the 1980 Grand Slam team — how did the current team compare? Who were the match winners? By how many points were England going to win? How did

England rate alongside the All Blacks? Rarely was there any mention of the Scottish team or the fact that England still had to play their final game, away from home in front of a partisan, vociferous and immensely patriotic crowd.

From afar, many would have thought that the Grand Slam had been won in England's first three games and that the result of the fourth match was a foregone conclusion! The combination of the arrogance of the English media in respect of their own team and the complete disregard of the abilities of the Scottish side served as a great inspiration for us. It was never going to be difficult to motivate the side when playing against the Auld Enemy, irrespective of what was at stake. If anything, I felt, we had to play things down and try to take our minds off the game — at the end of the day, it was just another rugby match.

The training and preparation for the game went well in the Wednesday and Thursday sessions so that, by the Friday 'Press session', all that was required was a brief 35-minute run-out. All the hard work had been done, not only in the days immediately before, but also in the training weekends stretching right back to October and November before the games against Fiji and Romania. We had also put in a lot of work during our blank weekend spent at Gleneagles and all the Sundays and other training days prior to the games against Ireland, France and Wales. The English game was going to be the culmination of all our hard work and preparation throughout the season. It would all come together in one 80-minute period. In the end the winner would take all. We had nothing to lose.

As match day dawned and the odds against a Scotland victory lengthened, there was a different feeling among the players. The usual nerves were present — one longed to be somewhere else, away from the pressure and the feeling of nausea. And yet not to have been involved would have been even worse.

The air of inevitability grew stronger and the fact that we were to be masters of our own destiny more tangible. And yet, despite the odds, the media reports and the butterflies, there was an aura of confidence throughout the team which had replaced the cautious optimism — a genuine belief that we could win this game.

Emotions ran high throughout the last-minute team talks. Big men wept as they realised once again the responsibilities of wearing the Thistle and playing in front of 50,000 Scots who would do anything to be in their places.

I can't remember my last few words to the players prior to leaving the dressing-room. But as we walked on to the pitch we were hit by a cacophony of sound which took the breath from our lungs.

By simply walking slowly from the dressing-room and for those first few yards on to the pitch it was our intention to impress on all present that we were approaching the game in a cool and clinical fashion. We wanted to underline that mood by walking slowly instead of coming out on to the pitch in our usual charge. We were throwing down the gauntlet.

Never have I experienced such an atmosphere at any sporting occasion. The sheer intensity of it was sustained for 80 minutes and more. The words of our newly adopted anthem, 'Flower of Scotland', could not have been more appropriate. We were the modern-day warriors and as we sang we felt the strength of an entire nation behind us.

The rest, as they say, is history.

A fast and furious 80 minutes of rugby left the English devastated. We had played with a hunger and an intensity such as I have never experienced or witnessed before in a Scotland jersey. With so much at stake it had felt as though we were condemned men and that our only pardon would come if the English were defeated. So it was. The taste of victory has never been sweeter.

What of the aftermath? The English players, many of whom a lot of us knew from the Lions' tour, accepted their defeat with great humility — something for which I respect them immensely. Perhaps they were victims of their own media hype, but I really don't think anything could have prepared them for what they had to face that day.

And the Scots? There is such a feeling of togetherness among all those involved, players, coaches and selectors, that the credit has to be shared — and we would want it no other way. The credit has to be shared not only at the playing, coaching and selectorial level but also with those who were at Murrayfield on 17 March and those millions of Scots beyond. Indeed it is only now, as one receives the dozens of letters daily, that one begins to fathom how far-reaching the implications are of Scotland having won the Grand Slam. The support that is always offered, has, and will continue to be, most gratefully appreciated.

There is a footnote to this foreword which opposing teams ought to heed when playing Scotland at home and which the English perhaps ignored at their peril — our patron, the Princess Royal, has never seen Scotland lose at Murrayfield.

D. M. B. SOLE
Edinburgh
27 March 1990

Chapter One

A SEASON TO RELISH

By BILL McMURTRIE

A SEASON TO RELISH

EMOTIONS WERE RUNNING HIGH on 17 March 1990. It was inescapable. Murrayfield was host to a unique match. For the first time England and Scotland were meeting in a head-on 'winner-take-all' contest. At stake were the Calcutta Cup, the Triple Crown, the Five Nations' Championship and the Grand Slam.

England were hyped by their flowing wins over Ireland (23-0), France (26-7) and Wales (34-6). The Border had been crossed with confidence. Their team were assured, though outwardly respectful of the Scots. The support blazed arrogance. 'Ready for your punishment?' asked an English voice. By marked contrast the Scots had steely resolve, players and support alike. The spirit of Bannockburn was in the air. Nothing would be more pleasing than to lay the proud usurper low, especially in a match of so much meaning. It was Jim Telfer's birthday, just as it had been on that day in 1984 when the Scots had completed their second Grand Slam, 59 years after the first. In 1984 he was coach, now he was assistant to the mastermind, Ian McGeechan, the architect of the Lions' comeback that cut down the Wallabies the previous year, and today Telfer was 50. What better reason had the Scots to celebrate? Also, greater recognition was accorded to 'Flower of Scotland', the Corries' ballad. It was the players' anthem and at their request two verses were to be sung instead of one. The closing words were evocative. The call was unmistakable for Scots to 'rise now and be the nation again that sent him homeward to think again'.

Not even in 1984, when France visited for the Grand Slam decider, had Murrayfield known such exhilaration, excitement, and expectancy. And into that arena the Scots marched. Where others ran, David Sole and his team walked. Unhurried, they filed on to the pitch, their eyes fixed ahead, ignoring the opposition. Theirs, though, was not a parade as if into a bullring. They had no arrogance of toreadors. Their gait had the assurance of elite troops striding to the battle-front. Was Bannockburn like that? The ploy, Sole's own idea, was as much a challenge as a New Zealand *haka* and they played with the single-minded purpose of the All Blacks.

17

For 80 minutes the commitment on both sides was unrelenting. The Scottish forwards, though, often had that extra nudge, not through heavier weight or superior height. They had the greater thirst for success. Out of their reserves they drew that little extra which had been latent in successive victories against Ireland, France and Wales.

So ended a memorable international season — six games, six wins, including victories against Fiji and Romania. Only once before had Scotland had such a run, when the 1925 Grand Slam was followed by wins over Wales and Ireland in 1926. This latest sequence was earned by tight-knit efficiency, each piece in the jig-saw fitted neatly into its place, not only on the field. Ian McGeechan and Jim Telfer, as coaches, were grandmasters of their game, outwitting especially the English in their preparation and planning. The pair were content to allow the Sassenachs to believe in their own invincibility though at the same time ensuring that they had everything right in their minds and those of their players. As McGeechan remarked in the immediate aftermath of the contest, big games are won by doing the small things well.

Bob Munro, convenor of the international selectors, was also an expert in the small items. Nothing was unimportant in the build-up. He cared for the detail and no one outside the squad and committee will ever fully appreciate the value of his role, quite apart from chairing selection.

McGeechan and Telfer, of course, had the personnel, a team fashioned to the coaches' template, and it helped greatly that injury did not upset the grand design. For each of the four championship matches, Scotland fielded the same XV. Never before had they done so. The only change was when Derek Turnbull had to replace Derek White after 28 minutes of the final match.

Even with the squad of 21, continuity was maintained almost to the end. Turnbull, John Allan, Alex Brewster, Greig Oliver and Douglas Wyllie stood by for all four matches and Peter Dods missed only the last game: because of a depressed cheekbone fracture the Gala full-back gave way to the 20-year-old Craig Redpath, one of Jim Telfer's young Turks from Melrose, the club who had deservedly won the double of the national championship and Border League.

Such a Grand Slam did not come together by accident. It was not just that Bob Munro and his five fellow selectors fell heir to 15 ideal players. The personnel had to be shaped and fired in the furnace of international competition. To seek the source of success one has to turn back to 1986, when six newcomers were introduced for the match against France at Murrayfield, the opening game in the championship. Gavin and Scott Hastings were among them, the first brothers to play together on their débuts for Scotland since George and William Neilson in 1891. Matt Duncan, Finlay Calder, Jeremy Campbell-Lamerton and David Sole were introduced on the same day, and four of those six were permanent, key figures in the Grand Slam. Only John Jeffrey of the 1990 team was already in place in 1986 and it has been round those five that Scotland have built.

Off the field, Derrick Grant took over from Jim Telfer in 1986. Ian McGeechan emerged as assistant coach, and over the past four years the

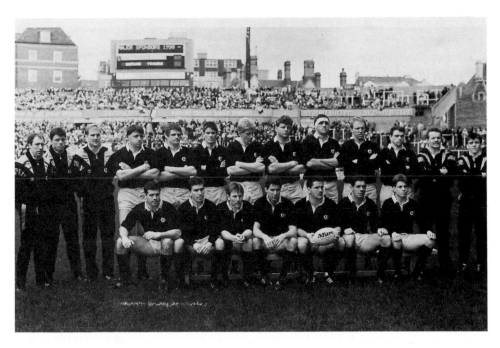

THE SCOTLAND LINE-UP AT CARDIFF WHEN THEY MET WELSH COACH RON WALDRON'S RE-CAST SIDE

GARY ARMSTRONG JUST MANAGES TO EVADE THE CLUTCHES OF HIS PREDATORY COUNTERPART. THE GAME IS
IRELAND V SCOTLAND AT LANSDOWNE ROAD THIS YEAR

influences have altered little. McGeechan, Telfer, and Grant will see Scotland through to the 1991 World Cup, along with Douglas Morgan.

Gavin Hastings kicked six penalty goals in an 18-17 victory against France on his début in 1986 and though the Scots lost in Cardiff, beaten 22-15 but scoring three tries to one, they won their other matches, shared the championship with France and then defeated Romania 33-18 in Bucharest. Twice in that season, against England and Romania, Gavin Hastings kicked 21 points, a Scottish record for an international.

1987 was not quite so profitable as 1986 had been. Wins against Ireland and Wales were balanced by defeats at Parc de Princes and Twickenham but the next major change in the Scottish team was on the horizon. The Rutherford-Laidlaw partnership was about to break up by accident.

John Rutherford and Roy Laidlaw were playing their 35th international together, a world record for half-backs, when Scotland entered the 1987 World Cup competition with a match against France in Christchurch. It was to be the pair's last in harness. Only seven minutes into the game, Rutherford, tackling Phillipe Sella, damaged knee ligaments so severely that he played little more rugby, even though he hung on in hope before he announced his retirement early the following year. By then, from the 1986 team, Colin Deans, Scotland's World Cup captain, and John Beattie had gone. Deans had decided that he should commit his career to paper and Beattie, like Rutherford, succumbed to injury.

Damian Cronin joined the incoming lists in 1988, Laidlaw's final year of international rugby, and the following season all but the last pieces fell into place with the introduction of Sean Lineen, Craig Chalmers, Gary Armstrong, Chris Gray and Kenneth Milne. Armstrong made his début against Australia and a 32-13 defeat by those Wallabies led to the promotion of the four others, a significant recasting if not quite so drastic as in 1986. Lineen, Boroughmuir's Kiwi recruit, son of an All Black, qualified through a grandfather from the Hebrides, and Chalmers was considered to have come of age only three months after his 20th birthday.

Lineen, Chalmers, Gray and Kenneth Milne had a memorable match for their débuts, Scotland beating Wales 23-7 at Murrayfield. Chalmers scored a try and a drop goal and for the same game Derek White switched to No 8 to join Finlay Calder, leading Scotland for the first time, and John Jeffrey. Thus was forged what was to be the breakaway trio so influential in the 1990 Grand Slam.

Kenneth Milne played only that one international beside his brother, Iain, renowned the world over as 'The Bear'. Injury removed the latter two days before the visit to Twickenham and so entered Paul Burnell for a demanding début at the age of 23, tender years for an international tight-head. The Grand Slam pack was complete.

Ireland, like Wales, lost at Murrayfield that season but all the Scots could achieve away from home was a draw at Twickenham. Defeat was suffered for the ninth successive time at Parc des Princes. Yet the Scots had done enough for nine of them to tour Australia with the Lions. Calder was captain and his fellow breakaway forwards were there, as were Sole, Armstrong, Chalmers, Dods and the Hastings brothers. Scotland provided both full-backs for the Lions: Gavin Hastings and the faithful Dods, the 1984 Grand Slam regular, who was back in Scotland's XV that season in the absence of the injured Anglo Scot.

It is now history how McGeechan and Calder, coach and captain, lifted the British Isles to victory in the series after the heavy loss of the first Test and unquestionably, as in 1984, the Scottish Lions benefited from the tour. Calder, however, did not continue as Scotland's captain. Sole took over in the flanker's absence for the October international against Fiji and though Calder was back to face Romania six weeks later, the prop remained in command.

Scotland had only one newcomer against Fiji — Tony Stanger was introduced on the right wing. The 21-year-old Hawick wing celebrated his début with two tries and he followed that with three against Romania. The last of the Grand Slam pieces was in place.

Victories against Fiji and Romania were comfortably won, by 38-17 and 32-0 respectively, but no one, especially with McGeechan emphasising the point, could delude himself that those matches were anything but contrasting warm-ups for the championship. Yet the games against Fiji and Romania had the advantage of drawing the team together, invaluable in helping the Scots through an uneasy game in Dublin. To win while not playing well was the sign of a potentially good team and the pieces fitted more easily against France, though it was only after Alain Carminati had been sent off for stamping on John Jeffrey that the Scots sailed away. That same day England swept Wales aside at Twickenham for their third win in three championship games.

Cardiff was always going to be difficult. Scotland had won there only three times since the war and Wales turned into an unknown quantity after John Ryan resigned as coach. Ron Waldron, introduced as successor, brought his Neath style and personnel with him and the new-look Welsh, though beaten, gave Scotland what Sole reckoned was as hard a game as he had known at Cardiff. So the stage was set for a contest which, unique in the prizes on offer, was truly the match of the century.

Once it was over and bequeathed to history, the Scots' initial relief quickly blossomed into satisfaction before swelling into joy. The campaign had been hard. It had not been spectacular. Modern Grand Slams are not won that way.

Yet it had its moments to savour long into the future: Sean Lineen's run to straighten the angle as the prelude to Derek White's first Dublin try; Iwan Tukalo's determination to make the goal-line, even on his hands and knees, for his try against France; Gary Armstrong's exploitation of rarely explored territory round the front of a lineout to make Damian Cronin's try against Wales; John Jeffrey's overbearing influence on that Cardiff match; the Jeffrey-Armstrong work to exploit fortune's sudden twist for Tony Stanger's try against England; and, though by no means less important than any try, that saving tackle by Scott Hastings on Rory Underwood.

21

28 October 1989 at Murrayfield

SCOTLAND 38

FIJI 17

A. G. Hastings (*London Scottish*)

Severo Koroduadua (*Police, Suva*)

A. G. Stanger (*Hawick*)
S. Hastings (*Watsonians*)
S. R. P. Lineen (*Boroughmuir*)
I. Tukalo (*Selkirk*)

T. Lovo (*QVS Old Boys, Suva*)
L. Erenavula (*Hyatt, Nadroga*)
N. Nadruku (*Hyatt, Nadroga*)
I. Waqawatu (*Army, Suva*)

C. M. Chalmers (*Melrose*)
G. Armstrong (*Jed-Forest*)

W. Serevi (*Nasinu, Rewa*)
L. Vasuvulagi (*Baravi, Nadroga*)

D. M. B. Sole (*Edinburgh Academicals*)
   captain
K. S. Milne (*Heriot's FP*)
A. P. Burnell (*London Scottish*)

M. Taga (*QVS Old Boys, Suva*)

S. Naivilawasa (*Police, Suva*)
S. Naituku (*Lomaiviti, Suva*)

C. A. Gray (*Nottingham*)
D. F. Cronin (*Bath*)

I. Savai (*QVS Old Boys, Suva*)
M. Rasari (*Army, Suva*)

J. Jeffrey (*Kelso*)
D. B. White (*London Scottish*)
G. R. Marshall (*Selkirk*)

P. Naruma (*Police, Suva*)
E. Teleni (*Army, Suva*) captain
A. Dere (*Army, Suva*)

Replacement:
G. A. E. Buchanan-Smith
(*London Scottish*) for Marshall
(67 minutes)

Tries:
Stanger (2)
A. G. Hastings
Tukalo
Milne
Gray

Tries:
Lovo
Rasari

Conversions:
A. G. Hastings (4)

Penalty goals:
A. G. Hastings (2)

Penalty goals:
Koroduadua (2)
Serevi

Referee: P. Robin (*France*)
Touch judges: R. Hourquet (*France*), A. Cuq (*France*)

DAVID SOLE joining the ranks of international captains, led Scotland by example in the victory over Fiji. No one in the world could be better in driving rugby than the Edinburgh prop was that day.

The Scots had no reason to fear that they had lost Finlay Calder, last season's commander and the Lions' general in the comeback to win the Test series against the Wallabies. Hardly had the game started than Sole was breenging through the opposition. Others responded, with Chris Gray and Kenneth Milne extending their contributions into scoring tries in a result that made a mockery of the 1991 World Cup seedings that placed Fiji ahead of Scotland. In the Fijians' only other Scottish match, three days earlier, they had fallen to Glasgow by 11-22 at Hughenden. There, too, frontal assault knocked the tourists back.

David Robertson, the Fijians' assistant coach, summed up Scotland's Murrayfield authority with a simple remark, though it was directed more at his own teams' needs: 'Obviously, we have to find a way of combating driving play.' He even suggested that the Scots in that respect reminded him of the All Blacks, a compliment, especially coming from a New Zealander.

Yet despite this being the basis for the Scots' expansive game in victory, with six tries to two, they needed domination at another level to launch their surge. They found it in a phase of lineout command which, though brief, was a prelude to the two tries that carried them from a tenuous three-point lead to 18-3 in the space of four minutes. In that time Scotland won six out of eight lineouts, a sudden turnabout when they had been outplayed, mainly by Ilaitia Savai, on the touch-line during the first quarter. Gray was the key figure in taking command, with Damian Cronin, John Jeffrey and Graham Marshall chipping in. All the more creditably, much of that success was achieved by countering Fiji's attempted shortened lineouts.

Jeffrey's lineout take released a surge up the right via Gary Armstrong, Sole and Marshall into Fiji's 22. Marshall gathered Milne's long throw-in at the next lineout, the inevitable Sole charged on, Marshall was there in support and Milne finished off with his first try for Scotland.

A Sean Lineen interception sent the Hastings brothers into the opposition 22 and, from the scrummage there, the Scots worked a mesmeric ploy more typical of France. Armstrong served, Craig Chalmers fed White and Armstrong looped the No 8 forward to send Tony Stanger over for the first of his two début tries, the young wing cutting inside off his right foot and accelerating for the goal-line. Gavin Hastings converted both tries, adding to his two earlier penalty goals. With two more conversions in the second half, as well as a try, he scored 18 points in the match.

Fiji had chances of their own but, as Robertson remarked afterwards, they lost good opportunities in the first half-hour. Inexperienced players, he said, took bad options. Indeed, the tourists might well have gone to a 7-3 lead when Isikeli Waqawatu chipped into the left corner. Armstrong's fingertips just denied Luke Erenavula and, between the Scots' two first-half tries, Erenavula, Noa Nadruku, Esala Teleni and Salaciele Naivilawasa broke from deep in their own half on a threat that Gavin Hastings and Iwan Tukalo closed down only in the home 22.

It was typical that Teleni was involved then. Like Sole, the Fijian captain led from the front and it was not the only time that Erenavula and Nadruku, centre partners in the Nadroga province's XV, forged space for themselves. Nadruku would attack at pace and, when halted, he had Erenavula at his shoulder.

Fiji's only first-half scores were two penalty goals by Severo Koroduadua. One was a prompt response to the Scots' first and the other, from more than 40 metres, cut the interval margin to 18-6.

Scotland's driving play continued in the second half, though it was 16 minutes after the interval before the lead stretched. A scrum close to the Fijian goal-line transformed into a rolling maul, with Gray at its core, and Armstrong's blind-side sortie let Stanger in past two failing tackles for his second try.

Waisale Serevi's 40-metre penalty goal cut Scotland to 22-9 but two more home tries followed in little more than five minutes. When another narrow-side attack by Armstrong and Stanger was thwarted, with the young right wing only just denied a third try, Gray swooped in to pick up and score and, from another close-range scrum, this time on the left, Armstrong's long, flat, rifling pass sent Gavin Hastings in beside the posts. It was a variation of Greg Martin's try for the Wallabies in the first Test against the Lions, a score of which four of the Scots had intimate memories. From that range, intruding full-backs such as Gavin Hastings are well nigh unstoppable. Armstrong's pass for that try was just another facet of the scope of his secure game. His service was ideal, he varied his play with the occasional kick, one with a long, probing touch-finder through a narrow channel, and he was around when needed in retreat.

Between the Gray and Hastings tries, both converted, Scotland were briefly down to 13 after a collision between the Selkirk pair, Marshall and Tukalo. The former, his forehead badly cut, was replaced by Adam Buchanan-Smith, the second of only three new caps Scotland needed this season. Tukalo soon returned, though not before Jeffrey, deputising on the left wing, had had a run to the corner. He was denied only by Erenavula, and afterwards Jeffrey could relish the thought of what, had he scored, Tukalo's reaction might have been.

Scotland led 34-9 with little more than ten minutes left, but Fiji were by no means finished. The tourists mustered their own version of driving assault for two tries, scores which had lessons for the Scots for later in the season. Teleni and the 18-stone Sairusi Naituku handled in the lead-up to both of the Fijian tries. Tomasi Lovo and Mesake Rasari were the scorers, though Scott Hastings was adamant that the former had put a foot in touch as he was tackled by Tukalo in the corner. Serevi missed both conversions and, in added time, the Scots had the last word in a series of assaults in which Jeffrey was involved three times. Lineen, Jeffrey, White and Cronin were denied in sharp succession, but at last perseverance paid off when a rucked ball let Scott Hastings put Tukalo away to twist over the line.

After the match, Ian McGeechan, Scotland's coach, complimenting the tourists, said: 'With Fiji you can't take anything for granted. They are big, strong men and if you give them space they have the ability, like the French, to use it. They are capable of keeping the ball alive when most other sides would die. From our point of view it was a creditable performance to deny them tries until the last five minutes.'

Conceding those tries reminded the Scots that they would have to play 80-minute rugby to succeed in the championship. Winners have no time for relaxation.

9 December 1989 at Murrayfield

SCOTLAND 32   ROMANIA 0

SCOTLAND 32	ROMANIA 0
A. G. Hastings (*London Scottish*)	M. Toader (*Dinamo Bucharest*)
A. G. Stanger (*Hawick*)	S. Chirila (*Politechnica Iasi*)
S. Hastings (*Watsonians*)	A. Lungu (*Dinamo Bucharest*)
S. R. P. Lineen (*Boroughmuir*)	G. Sava (*Baia Mare*)
W. L. Renwick (*London Scottish*)	B. Serban (*Steaua Bucharest*)
D. S. Wyllie (*Stewart's-Melville FP*)	G. Ignat (*Steaua Bucharest*)
G. Armstrong (*Jed-Forest*)	D. Neaga (*Dinamo Bucharest*)
D. M. B. Sole (*Edinburgh Academicals*) captain	G. Leonte (*Steaua Bucharest*)
K. S. Milne (*Heriot's FP*)	G. Ion (*Dinamo Bucharest*)
A. P. Burnell (*London Scottish*)	G. Dumitrescu (*Steaua Bucharest*)
C. A. Gray (*Nottingham*)	S. Ciorascu (*Baia Mare*)
D. F. Cronin (*Bath*)	C. Raducanu (*Dinamo Bucharest*)
J. Jeffrey (*Kelso*)	O. Sugar (*Baia Mare*)
D. B. White (*London Scottish*)	H. Dumitras (*Contactoare Buzau*) captain
F. Calder (*Stewart's-Melville FP*)	I. Doja (*Dinamo Bucharest*)

Tries:
Stanger (3)
Sole
White

Conversions:
A. G. Hastings (3)

Penalty goals:
A. G. Hastings (2)

Referee: S. R. Hilditch (*Ireland*)
Touch judges: O. E. Doyle (*Ireland*), B. W. Stirling (*Ireland*)

SCOTLAND'S VICTORY against Romania was unquestionably Derek White's match. The London Scottish No 8 was the dominant figure even in a game in which Tony Stanger scored three tries to add to the two he had on his début against Fiji. Not for many a day has a Scottish No 8 imposed himself on an international as White did against the Romanians.

His scrummage pick-ups were the launch pads for one particular phase of percussion play in the first half, as Scotland stepped down the field almost in the manner of grid-iron football. He picked up from three successive scrums and the development of each ploy was different from the others despite the personnel being mainly the same. Gary Armstrong twice played off the No 8, once drawing the support with him into a ruck and later linking with White and Finlay Calder on a more progressive thrust. Between those two plays, Sean Lineen was White's liaison. The total gain was nearly 50 metres, from well inside the Scots' own half to deep in the Romanian 22.

Nothing came of that sortie but a subsequent White pick-up did produce a try, the No 8 going off on his own from a scrum about ten metres out. Once he had shrugged off Ovidiu Sugar's tackle, the gap opened up for a rehearsal for the more crucial try against Ireland eight weeks later.

Victory over Romania was a landmark in Scottish rugby history. Not for more than 25 years had Scotland shut out opponents in international rugby. Scotland's 10-0 victory over France in January 1964 was their last international win without conceding a point and the second of three successive Murrayfield matches in which visitors failed to score. Eleven months earlier Scotland had beaten Ireland 3-0 and the win over France was followed a fortnight later by the famous no-score draw with Wilson Whineray's All Blacks. After the win over Romania, however, the Scots did not have to wait so long for their next shut-out. Their following match at Murrayfield, little more than two months later, was the 21-0 win over France.

Romania's zero pleased David Sole, the Scots' captain, almost as much as the five tries his team scored. Secure defence three times held out the visitors encamped on the Scottish goal-line, however briefly. It was handy practice for the onslaughts that were to follow, especially by Wales and England.

Sole, however, was disappointed in certain aspects of the win against Romania, principally that the Scots did not play to their ideal for the full 80 minutes. All five tries were scored inside 25 minutes, beginning just before the interval.

Ian McGeechan, Scotland's coach, was pleased that the team were scoring tries, 11 in all over the games against Fiji and Romania, and he sympathised with Sole that the impetus had not been maintained in the last quarter of an hour. 'In a half-empty international stadium it's not easy to keep it up,' McGeechan remarked, referring to the poor attendance of 20,000. No one could voice that complaint for Murrayfield's two subsequent internationals, each with a full house of 54,000.

Calder, an absentee from the match against Fiji, was back against Romania, renewing his happy liaison with White and John Jeffrey. Craig Chalmers, however, was missing, as was Iwan Tukalo. Both were injured. Douglas Wyllie

28

HALF-BACK PARTNERSHIP... GARY ARMSTRONG AND CRAIG CHALMERS PLAYED A PIVOTAL ROLE IN SCOTLAND'S GRAND SLAM TRIUMPH

A GONG FOR FINLAY. THE BRITISH LIONS SKIPPER WAS AWARDED THE OBE IN THE 1990 NEW YEAR'S HONOURS LIST

returned for his tenth cap in place of Chalmers at stand-off and Lindsay Renwick made his début on the left wing. As December turned into January, even with the opening championship international not until February, the Melrose stand-off's knee injury became increasingly alarming. A minor operation rectified it and Chalmers was healed in plenty of time for the visit to Dublin.

Scotland's opening try against Romania was not until just before the interval. Yet even before then they had showed willing to be expansive and varied. They were working their game out.

Especially early on, Chris Gray did well at the front of the lineout, not only on Scottish throws. His domination for one short spell provided a platform, when coupled with the Scots' mainly secure scrummaging and White's persistent threat, and, though nothing came directly from Gray's takes, the possession he won did much to help the home team settle into the match.

Scotland might have fallen behind before they struck for the first time via Stanger. Gelu Ignat missed two penalties but the Scots were defensively as secure as they had been for a long time. Armstrong and the breakaway forwards had a grip of the close-quarter game.

Once in each half the Romanians unavailingly hammered the Scottish goal-line. A series of five-metre scrums, prompted by Ignat's delicious grub kick to the right corner, came to naught against the dark-blue wall, and two successive tapped-penalty ploys were also thwarted, though Haralambie Dumitras and Gheorghe Dumitrescu could have been only inches away.

Responding to the first of those Romanian assaults, Gray's take at a close-range lineout and Kenneth Milne's link almost procured the first Scottish try. The persistent Armstrong, however, was turned on to his back as he was driven over. From the ensuing scrum, he attempted the ploy that had produced a try for Gavin Hastings against Fiji in October, the scrum-half firing a long, flat pass to the full-back who was intruding at maximum revs. Marcel Toader, alive to man-to-man marking, denied his opposite number but Calder swooped in to regenerate the attack. Douglas Wyllie, too, was stopped, but Scott Hastings slipped the vital pass away for Stanger, who still had to beat two opponents before he planted the ball for a try as he was tackled into the right corner post.

Gavin Hastings converted that try and White's score to add to his opening penalty goal in 26 minutes and, after the second of Romania's goal-line sieges, the Scottish full-back was involved again, surging out of two tackles at halfway. His pass was blocked but the inevitable White gathered the rebound for a galloping run into the 22. Lineen, continuing the sortie, was denied in the right corner but Stanger was there to pick up and score.

Again Gavin Hastings converted and, after Sugar had departed with a head injury — replaced immediately by Marian Motoc — Sole strode away from a free kick around halfway to release Stanger and Armstrong on a passing exchange. The scrum-half did well to slip the ball out of a tackle, to send the young wing in for his third try of the match.

Gavin Hastings failed with that conversion but soon added his second penalty goal before Lineen's long pass, missing out the intruding full-back, fired Scott Hastings and Renwick close to the left corner. Romania were penalised in the tackle there and Sole surged off on his own to score. Like Milne's score, it was the captain's first international try.

Scotland then went off the boil. The problems that had afflicted their game in the first half were again apparent. Not the least of those was that the Scots had won only one of the last 11 lineouts as Sandu Ciorascu dominated the touch-line. Ciorascu also had Romania's last chance of a try when the admirable lock-forward almost reached the line from George Sava's garryowen. Fortune smiled again when Ignat had his third penalty miss.

Scotland's victory was their fourth in five internationals against Romania. The margin was the widest, beating the 55-28 win in the 1987 World Cup contest in Dunedin.

After such a hefty defeat the Romanians might have wished to retreat as quickly as possible behind what then remained of the Iron Curtain. Instead, before attending the official dinner, they had a happy hour relaxing at Goldenacre as Heriot's guests. A Romanian jersey was among the trophies for Heriot's centenary showcase, though one Goldenacre wag suggested that he would have preferred if the visitors had left Ciorascu behind. Little did that Herioter know that even then Ciorascu's lock partner, Cristian Raducanu, was preparing to defect. The Romanians were one short when they flew home the following day.

3 February 1990 at Lansdowne Road

IRELAND 10

K. Murphy (*Constitution*)

M. J. Kiernan (*Dolphin*)
B. J. Mullin (*Blackrock College*)
D. G. Irwin (*Instonians*)
K. D. Crossan (*Instonians*)

B. A. Smith (*Oxford University*)
L. F. P. Aherne (*Lansdowne*)

J. J. Fitzgerald (*Young Munster*)

J. P. McDonald (*Malone*)
D. C. Fitzgerald (*Lansdowne*)

D. G. Lenihan (*Constitution*)
W. A. Anderson (*Dungannon*)
  captain

P. M. Matthews (*Wanderers*)
N. P. Mannion (*Corinthians*)
P. J. O'Hara (*Sunday's Well*)

Replacement:
P. C. Collins (*London Irish*) for
O'Hara (38 minutes)

Tries:
J. J. Fitzgerald

Penalty goal:
Kiernan (2)

SCOTLAND 13

A. G. Hastings (*London Scottish*)

A. G. Stanger (*Hawick*)
S. Hastings (*Watsonians*)
S. R. P. Lineen (*Boroughmuir*)
I. Tukalo (*Selkirk*)

C. M. Chalmers (*Melrose*)
G. Armstrong (*Jed-Forest*)

D. M. B. Sole (*Edinburgh Academicals*)
  captain
K. S. Milne (*Heriot's FP*)
A. P. Burnell (*London Scottish*)

C. A. Gray (*Nottingham*)
D. F. Cronin (*Bath*)

J. Jeffrey (*Kelso*)
D. B. White (*London Scottish*)
F. Calder (*Stewart's-Melville FP*)

Tries:
White (2)

Conversion:
Chalmers

Penalty goal:
Chalmers

Referee: C. Norling (*Wales*)
Touch judges: W. D. Bevan (*Wales*), L. J. Peard (*Wales*)

YOU'RE NOT GOING ANYWHERE, PAL! GAVIN HASTINGS HANGS ON FOR GRIM LIFE AGAINST THE WELSH AT CARDIFF

OFFSIDE? SURELY NOT. CALDER GATHERING UP SCRAPS AT A WELSH LINEOUT

SCOTLAND'S CENTRE PAIRING SCOTT HASTINGS (TOP) AND SEAN LINEEN (BOTTOM). THE DYNAMIC DUO PROVED TO BE AN
IDEAL COUPLING . THROUGHOUT THE GRAND SLAM SEASON LINEEN'S DIRECT RUNNING AND INTELLIGENT USE OF ANGLES,
COUPLED WITH HASTINGS' ALL ROUND ABILITY AND DEVASTATING TACKLING, WERE A MAJOR ASSET

BALL WATCHING. CHRIS GRAY, FINLAY CALDER AND DAVID SOLE

SEAN LINEEN, SCOTLAND'S KIWI CENTRE WITH THE IRISH MONIKER AND ARCHITECT OF THE GRAND SLAM VICTORY, COACH
IAN MCGEECHAN

MONARCH OF THE GLEN? PERHAPS NOT, BUT CERTAINLY DAVID SOLE REIGNED SUPREME THROUGHOUT SCOTLAND'S
GRAND SLAM SEASON

THE START OF A HISTORIC SEASON FOR SKIPPER DAVID SOLE AND SCOTLAND, WITH A MURRAYFIELD VICTORY OVER THE FIJIANS

CHICKEN CHASSEUR. A FRENCH COCKEREL MAKES FRANTIC EFFORTS TO EVADE FINLAY CALDER AS THE BIG FLANKER BREENGES FOR THE LINE DURING THE MURRAYFIELD DEFEAT OF THE FRENCH

FORMATION MARKING AS THE FRENCH DEFENCE CLOSES IN ON GARY ARMSTRONG. SEAN LINEEN AND JOHN JEFFREY ARE ABOUT TO JOIN THE FRAY

ARMSTRONG AGAIN GETS HIS PASS AWAY DESPITE THE CLOSE ATTENTION OF THE FRENCH
ALAIN CARMINATI, THE FAIR-HAIRED BACK-ROW PLAYER, LATER RECEIVED HIS MARCHING ORDERS FOR A BRUTAL FOUL ON JEFFREY

SCOTLAND No 8 DEREK WHITE, ALTHOUGH RETIRING HURT IN THE CALCUTTA CUP MATCH, WAS AN INVALUABLE MEMBER OF THE GRAND SLAM TEAM

IT'S MY BALL. FINLAY CALDER HAS NO INTENTION OF GIVING UP POSSESSION DESPITE DESPERATE FRENCH ATTEMPTS TO MAKE HIM DO SO

DAMIAN CRONIN RESISTS THE FRENCH ADVANCES. JOHN JEFFREY AND FINLAY CALDER DEAL WITH LAURENT RODRIGUEZ

SCOTLAND'S VISIT to Lansdowne Road did not have auspicious portents. The flight out of Edinburgh, two days before the match, was delayed for an hour as Dublin Airport had been closed because of severe gales and even when the Scots were in the air all was not well. A door was found not to have been properly shut and the aircraft had to return to Edinburgh. Supporters had even worse tales of travelling by air and sea. Moreover, Ian McGeechan, Scotland's coach, was not in Dublin. A virus had laid him low and Jim Telfer took charge, assisted by Douglas Morgan. The impact of the enforced change, however, was cushioned by pre-planning. The Scots, preparing for the 1991 World Cup, had already appointed an interchangeable coaching team of McGeechan, Morgan, Telfer, and Derrick Grant. Morgan stepped easily into his new, temporary role.

As for the game itself, it was never going to be easy, as David Sole, Scotland's captain, admitted afterwards. The circumstances were not right, quite apart from it being an away match. Ireland had had hard matches against New Zealand and England, though they lost both, and the Scots did not overlook the fact that Ireland were down by only 0-7 at Twickenham before England piled on 16 points in the last ten minutes. The Irish, the Scots recognised, would have been sharpened by that Twickenham match only two weeks earlier whereas Scotland had had two months since their win over Romania.

Victory at Lansdowne Road was achieved in a match that was certainly not one of rugby's classics. It was a game for the Scots to have well out of the way. They won while not playing as well as they could. No hint was to be seen of Grand Slam champions in the making, though the margin was less than it ought to have been, and the result generated a unanimous feeling of relief among the visitors on and off the field.

It was a rare win for Scotland away from home and that was excuse enough for taking a measure of pleasure from the result. Sole summed that up after the match. In a career at that time stretching for 22 internationals he had not previously known victory in a championship match outside Murrayfield. The last such one was four years ago, also in Dublin, and Sole missed that because of injury.

This time the Scots hung millstones round their necks by failing to convert phases of first-half pressure into points. Three times they went close but Ireland led 7-0 at the interval. Immediately after Michael Kiernan's opening penalty goal, Sole and Kenneth Milne essayed a blind-side thrust off a rucked ball on the right for Craig Chalmers to send Scott Hastings almost to the goal-line, but the centre was denied by Ken Murphy. Less than ten minutes later Gavin Hastings struck a penalty kick neatly into the left corner, prompting a siege, though only brief, and, as the first half was closing with Ireland still leading by three points, a Chalmers garryowen trapped Murphy before Chalmers and Scott Hastings all but set up a try for Tony Stanger. From none of those sorties could Scotland keep the screws turned tight. They had not the necessary consistency on the touch-line despite Chris Gray's sterling efforts to catch and drive. Willie Anderson and Noel Mannion ruled the lineout for Ireland in the first half.

As the championship progressed, however, the Scottish lineout play was to improve. The Scots added to their armoury with each match and, by the time they played the Grand Slam decider against England, they were as streetwise as any wily, old campaigner. Gray, introduced to the national team in 1989, exemplified the Scots' development: by the Dublin match, his emergence as an ideal international lock, not only as front jumper, was noticeable. He has utility value in the loose with the ability to be in the right places, as in the first ten minutes at Lansdowne Road. At one point he was back to assist Iwan Tukalo turn an Irish threat and the lock was also on hand when Scott Hastings almost scored.

Gray and the breakaway forwards provided the cement that bound Scotland together. The foundation was the secure defence, with Gavin Hastings typically solid under any high ball from Brian Smith. Often in the three subsequent championship matches were those words to be echoed, complimenting the back-row trio, Finlay Calder, Derek White, and John Jeffrey, as well as marvelling at the admirable defence.

White scored two crucial tries in the Dublin match, the first cutting back Ireland's half-time lead and the second putting Scotland ahead for the first time, whereas Calder and Jeffrey responded to the challenge that had been thrown at them when they were selected in the junior team in the national trial a month earlier. The sight of Calder driving and surging must have raised others' spirits. He also did much in Scotland's second-half lineout improvement, as did Jeffrey. The Scots, indeed, all but broke even on the touch-line after the interval and that was all the more commendable when Ireland had the throw-ins in a ratio of slightly wider than three to one. It was, at least, a hopeful sign.

Against those plus points had to be set more worrying factors: the scrummage was not so forceful as the Irish, though the Scots once generated a hefty shunt late on; Chalmers and Gary Armstrong were not in tune with one another, and the kicking from hand by Chalmers and Gavin Hastings was not consistently accurate enough to exert regular pressure on Murphy, a brave, competent, secure full-back. A blustery, swirling wind did not help, though Smith had no trouble in firing his mortars.

Hastings also missed three first-half penalty shots at goal and, for the first time in 21 internationals, he failed to score. Chalmers miscued an attempted drop goal that would have cut Ireland's lead to 10-9 midway in the second half but the stand-off, taking over the place-kicking from Gavin Hastings, followed up with a penalty goal after a charge by Calder and White. John McDonald was the culprit, playing the ball on the ground after his tackle on the No 8.

Kiernan kicked two out of four. One of his misses was from five metres inside his own half but the other was from less than half that distance. It would have drawn Ireland belatedly level and Scottish eyes could hardly bear to watch that kick. His first penalty goal rewarded a lineout peel by Mannion off Philip Matthews, and his second, responding to White's first try, was the result of a refereeing mistake by Clive Norling. It should have been a free kick not a penalty. With Ireland leading 7-6 after 52 minutes, Norling awarded a scrummage free-kick, and the Scots charged as soon as Fergus Aherne placed the ball on the

DAMIAN CRONIN . . . THE BATH LOCK'S GAME HAS IMPROVED TREMENDOUSLY IN THE PAST COUPLE OF YEARS

ground. The scrum-half made a hurried pass to Smith and Jeffrey blocked the stand-off's attempted drop goal. Norling, however, ruled that the Scots had charged too soon and he awarded a penalty kick ten metres forward. That was his error, regardless of the right or wrong of his ruling against the charge. The law states that the additional penalty for an infringement in such circumstances is another free kick (not a penalty) advanced ten metres. Norling later acknowledged his mistake and the Kiernan penalty goal, though taking Ireland to 10-6, was not as disastrous as it might have been. The Scots edged back and overtook the Irish with White's second try.

Luck, however, seemed to be with the Irish after they had broken a Scottish surge late in the first half. The home team countered via Murphy and Keith Crossan and misfortune followed misfortune for the Scots. Armstrong tried to hack into touch, the ball rebounded off Stanger, Crossan chased into the 22, Armstrong's scrummage clearance was partially blocked, Crossan fired Mannion at the line, Anderson also had a drive and, when the ball squirted out of the goal-line ruck, John Fitzgerald pounced for the try that took Ireland to 7-0 after 37 minutes. Before Kiernan's conversion miss, Pat O'Hara retired with an eye injury and Paul Collins took over at wing-forward.

Scotland responded soon after the interval. Scott Hastings and Tukalo attacked the left and, from a swift ruck ball, Sean Lineen's straightening run let Jeffrey send White over. Chalmers converted and a penalty goal each by Kiernan and Chalmers left the margin at just one point going into the last quarter. But an assault by Tukalo, Gavin Hastings and Jeffrey to the line set the example for the Scots' finale, and the winning try, when it came, almost had an inevitability about it.

Calder, Gray, Armstrong, and Calder again carried the game into the Irish 22. Armstrong was denied, as were Calder and Lineen, and when White ran to the narrow side from his own scrummage pick-up, the defence opened for him as it had done for his try against Romania in December. Relief was almost audible, even more so when Kiernan missed that late penalty.

17 February 1990 at Murrayfield

SCOTLAND 21   FRANCE 0

A. G. Hastings (*London Scottish*)   S. Blanco (*Biarritz*)

A. G. Stanger (*Hawick*)   P. Hontas (*Biarritz*)
S. Hastings (*Watsonians*)   P. Sella (*Agen*)
S. R. P. Lineen (*Boroughmuir*)   F. Mesnel (*Racing Club*)
I. Tukalo (*Selkirk*)   P. Lagisquet (*Bayonne*)

C. M. Chalmers (*Melrose*)   D. Camberabero (*Beziers*)
G. Armstrong (*Jed-Forest*)   H. Sanz (*Narbonne*)

D. M. B. Sole (*Edinburgh Academicals*)   M. Pujolle (*Nice*)
  captain
K. S. Milne (*Heriot's FP*)   L. Armary (*Lourdes*)
A. P. Burnell (*London Scottish*)   P. Ondarts (*Biarritz*)

C. A. Gray (*Nottingham*)   T. Devergie (*Nimes*)
D. F. Cronin (*Bath*)   O. Roumat (*Dax*)

J. Jeffrey (*Kelso*)   J-M. Lhermet (*Montferrand*)
D. B. White (*London Scottish*)   L. Rodriguez (*Dax*) captain
F. Calder (*Stewart's-Melville FP*)   A. Carminati (*Beziers*)

Tries:
Tukalo
Calder

Conversions:
Chalmers (2)

Penalty goals:
Chalmers (2)
A. G. Hastings

Referee: F. A. Howard (*England*)
Touch judges: I. M. Bullerwell (*England*), E. F. Morrison (*England*)

FRENCH INDISCIPLINE has been notorious on the rugby field. Under pressure they can lose their cool, as they did in the 1984 Grand Slam decider against Scotland, though no single incident could have been worse and more costly than Alain Carminati's brutal stamping on John Jeffrey's head in the countries' 1990 contest. Fred Howard sent the 23-year-old Beziers forward off and Carminati was subsequently suspended from rugby for 30 weeks.

After his dismissal Scotland, their noses already in front, pulled away with two tries to a comfortable victory. It was the Scots' sixth successive Murrayfield win over France.

A change in the wind helped too. Scotland had made too little of the gusting blast that they had had in their favour in the first half. At the interval they were only three points up from a Gavin Hastings penalty goal but, instead of having to face the elements in defending such a slender lead, they found that the wind had swung and eased.

Laurent Rodriguez, replacing the deposed Pierre Berbizier as the French captain, had every reason to regret his decision to give Scotland the wind in the first half. He had all the more cause to hang his head in horror when Howard sent Carminati off eight minutes into the second half. Thereafter the Scots tightened their grasp on the game. It was, too, their most substantial margin in 25 Murrayfield games against the French and it squared the overall series at 29 each.

Jeffrey, with cuts on his left ear and chin from Carminati's boot, was happily restored and Craig Chalmers kicked the penalty goal. David Sole, Scotland's captain, described it as the turning point. 'The French heads went down. Ours came up,' he said afterwards, though he admitted to the relief of feeling the wind change at half-time.

Gavin Hastings, secure in all the full-back essentials, proved the significance of that wind-veer with a huge clearing kick early in the second half. The Scots pressed on, Gavin Hastings powered in intrusion, Tony Stanger and Chris Gray drove on and it was at the stoppage there that Carminati lost his cool.

Over the first half the Scots did more than enough to deserve to have been substantially ahead and they should have had more, even if only on penalty goals. Gavin Hastings struck two wide, one from barely 15 metres out, and Chalmers hit a post with his sighting shot before he went on to score ten second-half points with two conversions and his two penalty goals that sandwiched tries by Finlay Calder and Iwan Tukalo. The stand-off's second conversion was with a beautifully struck kick from tight on the left touch-line.

Scott Hastings and Tukalo came close to first-half tries, each just beaten as he chased through in the sequel to a deep kick that twisted in the wind, teasing Serge Blanco. Gary Armstrong struck the first and Gavin Hastings the second and each time the French full-back was engulfed. A similar kick by Chalmers enticed indecision between Blanco and Pierre Hontas as Tony Stanger followed through. The covering Patrice Lagisquet saved them. After the match Ian McGeechan, Scotland's coach, acknowledged the difficulties his team had in breaking the

38

JOHN JEFFREY, c 1982

French in the first half. He expected a containment game when Rodriguez had conceded the weather advantage from the toss.

As background to that pressure, pleasing McGeechan, the Scottish lineout game improved markedly from Dublin two weeks earlier. Chris Gray was outstanding at the front, his two-handed catches the catalyst for forceful driving mauls, and Damian Cronin, outplaying Olivier Roumat, was much more effective than he had been in any of the season's three previous internationals. Beside them, Sole was the master in sweeping and peeling. Scotland also scored advantage off the unity and understanding that Jeffrey, Derek White and Calder had developed. The threesome magnetised support even before their opposite numbers were depleted by Carminati's departure. Jean-Marc Lhermet, making his début, was denied the scope he had enjoyed in the B international against the Scots in Oyonnax four weeks earlier.

Yet more than once Scottish hearts momentarily sank. Chalmers had to effect hand-trips to deny each of the escaping wings, and Phillipe Sella could only knock on as he chased into goal from a Didier Camberabero up-and-under.

Camberabero missed two penalties in the third quarter, the second from no more than 30 metres, but, between those French failures, Scotland at last found the way through after 58 minutes, countering after Blanco had been thwarted running into the home half. Sean Lineen's long pass left Tukalo with working space, the wing chased his own long kick to catch Henri Sanz in the French 22, Scott Hastings followed up to trap Hontas and, when Lineen and Camberabero appeared to overshoot the ball in goal, Calder pounced for a try. Lineen claimed it as his first for Scotland. Howard, however, later removed any doubt by confirming that he awarded the try to 'the second Scot' — Calder.

Five minutes after that score Blanco, harassed by Lineen, fluffed his catch under a Chalmers garryowen. Lineen and Chalmers swung long passes left for Tukalo's tenth international try, a score in which true grit was as vital an ingredient as pace. The wing broke Hontas's tackle, staggered on, almost on hands and knees, and planted the ball over the line as Thierry Devergie arrived too late.

A fourth goal by Chalmers followed in five more minutes and only then did the French force the Scots on to retreat. Even that late the awareness was alive enough to earn Scotland their sixth shut-out in 61 matches against France. After the 32-0 win over Romania it was the second successive Murrayfield match in which Scotland had not conceded a score.

After the match Howard, English rugby's leading referee described Carminati's dismissal, recounting how he had seen the forward's knee 'come up almost to chest height' before the boot came down on the defenceless Jeffrey. The referee's revulsion was unrestrained as he scrolled through his vocabulary for adjectives to substantiate his horror at the incident. Jacques Fouroux, the French coach, was severe in his criticism of Carminati. So was Albert Ferrasse, president of the French Rugby Federation, who, addressing the referee at the post-match dinner, said: 'You did what you had to do. I thank you.'

To deal with the French forward's dismissal a disciplinary hearing was

40

convened by the Five Nations' Championship committee at Edinburgh Airport on the morning after the international. The venue was for the convenience of both Carminati, who had an afternoon flight to Toulouse, and Sir Ewart Bell, the former president of the Irish Rugby Football Union who flew in from Belfast via London to chair the meeting. It would have been held on the evening of the match had a flight been available for Sir Ewart.

As is the practice in such matters, the neutral chairman was joined by a representative from each side in the match. Gordon Masson, vice-president of the Scottish Rugby Union and one of the country's two delegates to the international board, and Francis Senegas, secretary-general of the French federation, sat in judgment along with Sir Ewart, and Bob Weighill, the championship secretary, was there as well. Carminati's suspension of 30 weeks was two less than the penalty imposed on Kevin Moseley, the Welsh forward whom the same Howard sent off during the Cardiff international against France the previous month.

With his dismissal Carminati's reputation caught up with him. When Scots first encountered him, playing for the French Barbarians four years earlier, they marked him down as one with a temperament that could land him in bother. Nor had Carminati heeded Howard's dismissal of Moseley. The warning ought to have been obvious to anyone but a hermit.

Carminati was the 16th player (the third Frenchman) to be sent off in an international, though only the second at Murrayfield. Colin Meads, the New Zealand forward, was the first to be dismissed there. That was in 1967 and he was only the second in nearly 100 years of international rugby. Such incidents have increased in recent times. All but six of the 16 have been in the past ten years and Howard, though no hanging judge, has dealt with three of them. As well as Moseley and Carminati, the Englishman dismissed David Codey, the Australian forward, in the Rotorua match against Wales to decide third place in the 1987 World Cup.

A rise in the rate of dismissals can be interpreted as showing an increase in foul play in international rugby but that view has to be taken parallel with the recognition that referees are more willing to weed out the thugs. Authority showed its support with the bans imposed on Moseley and Carminati.

THE FLOWERING OF SCOTLAND

3 February 1990 at Cardiff Arms Park

WALES 9   SCOTLAND 13

WALES 9	SCOTLAND 13
P. H. Thorburn (*Neath*)	A. G. Hastings (*London Scottish*)
M. R. Hall (*Cardiff*)	A. G. Stanger (*Hawick*)
M. G. Ring (*Cardiff*)	S. Hastings (*Watsonians*)
A. G. Bateman (*Neath*)	S. R. P. Lineen (*Boroughmuir*)
A. Emyr (*Swansea*)	I. Tukalo (*Selkirk*)
D. W. Evans (*Cardiff*)	C. M. Chalmers (*Melrose*)
R. N. Jones (*Swansea*) captain	G. Armstrong (*Jed-Forest*)
B. R. Williams (*Neath*)	D. M. B. Sole (*Edinburgh Academicals*) captain
K. H. Phillips (*Neath*)	K. S. Milne (*Heriot's FP*)
J. D. Pugh (*Neath*)	A. P. Burnell (*London Scottish*)
P. T. Davies (*Llanelli*)	C. A. Gray (*Nottingham*)
G. O. Llewellyn (*Neath*)	D. F. Cronin (*Bath*)
M. A. Perego (*Llanelli*)	J. Jeffrey (*Kelso*)
M. A. Jones (*Neath*)	D. B. White (*London Scottish*)
R. G. Collins (*Cardiff*)	F. Calder (*Stewart's-Melville FP*)

Replacement:
A. Clement (*Swansea*) for Evans
(52 minutes)

Try: **Try:**
Emyr   Cronin

Conversion:
Thorburn

Penalty goal: **Penalty goals:**
Thorburn   Chalmers (3)

Referee: R. Hourquet (*France*)
Touch judges: R. Robin (*France*), A. Ceccon (*France*)

42

FOR THE THIRD SUCCESSIVE MATCH, Scotland had to catch opposition on the rebound from a hefty defeat by England. Wales had lost 6-34 at Twickenham two weeks earlier but that was not the only influence on Scottish minds. John Ryan had resigned as Welsh coach after that drubbing. His had been an unimpressive record of seven defeats in nine games and Wales turned instead to Ron Waldron, coach of Neath, the most successful club in the principality.

Waldron brought his own men and his Neath style with him to try to turn the tide. Six changes were made from the XV beaten at Twickenham. The whole front row were from Neath, as were four others. Two of the Neath seven, Allan Bateman and Brian Williams, were newcomers and so was Mark Perego, the Llanelli flanker.

Williams, the Neath loose head, did not conform to the modern concept of a prop forward. At six feet one inch but only 13 stone 10 pounds, he was a complete contrast to Jeremy Pugh, the club's tight head — a lager glass to a Toby jug — but, however unbalanced the front row appeared, they looked lively in practice at the Welsh National Sports Centre in Cardiff on the Thursday evening before the international. Waldron, obviously, was keeping faith with his Neath style of pack mobility. The scrummage was to be a starting point rather than an end in itself.

In such circumstances the hope was that Scotland would command the scrums more than enough to lay the foundation for victory, and so it proved, at least in the first half of that prediction. Rarely in a modern championship international has one country dominated another so much in the scrummage, but the huge advantage was not reflected in the Scots' winning margin. Instead, as in the February victories against Ireland and France, Scotland suffered the agonies of uneasy passages. To win by just four points, with one try apiece, was far less than the Scots deserved. They had won three championship matches without firing on all cylinders and their best, hopefully, was to come against England.

Scotland's front row stated their scrummage case early on with Paul Burnell taking one against the head. The hint, though, was that Gary Armstrong had helped by upsetting the put-in by Robert Jones. Whatever the rights or wrongs, Scotland had stamped authority and Wales could not counter it. Jones could have helped the Welsh cause with the sharper put-in that the Neath front row were used to. A quick feed and fast delivery would have eased the pressure but Jones was still trapped between the old Ryan emphasis on scrummaging and the new Waldron ideal.

With the Scottish scrum turning the screws, John Jeffrey could lie off at will and, even in the seven minutes of withering Welsh assault just before the interval, the Kelso forward was able to stand aside as guard. White provided willing assistance against the unimaginative persistence with which Wales launched Mark Jones from scrummage pick-ups.

Jeffrey, White, Finlay Calder and Gary Armstrong were the solid wall against which the Welsh efforts foundered. Sean Lineen and Scott Hastings each made memorable tackles as well but it was the breakaway forwards' experience that tied the defence together. The catalyst for Scotland's latter moments: they were sharp in retreat and alive enough to turn defence into attack, none more so than Jeffrey, who extended his habit of playing well at Cardiff. He was the outstanding figure in the 1986 game, even in defeat, and two months later he had a memorable return to Cardiff for the International Rugby Football Board centenary match. The Cardiff air, it seems, is good for him.

Jeffrey himself, however, could pay respects to what was achieved by the front five. Sole had Pugh under so much pressure that the Welsh tight-head buckled too often for an international prop and Williams found that agricultural strength alone could not carry him through against a scrummager of Burnell's fast-growing reputation. The new loose-head's back was constantly arched in the scrum, though his mobility in the loose was unimpaired.

Scotland were almost as dominant on the touch-line as they were in the scrum. Damian Cronin signalled that command by winning the first two lineouts and thereafter he all but eclipsed Gareth Llewellyn. There, too, the inevitable Jeffrey was as much a key figure as anyone, not only taking the ball behind the middle jumpers but also in his support as the link for Cronin's try, the game's opening score after 16 minutes. Armstrong cut round the front of a lineout, Jeffrey drove on from support, Sole was there as well and Cronin was up to score. The Bath lock was delighted with his second try for Scotland. His 1989 score against Ireland at Murrayfield would always be special as his first try in international rugby but the Cardiff one, he acknowledged, was more important in the context of the match.

Gavin Hastings, kicking from tight on the left touch-line, missed the conversion and Paul Thorburn immediately replied with a goal from an offside penalty. Craig Chalmers, however, stretched the Scots' lead with two such scores. Phil Davies conceded the first by stamping at a ruck and Mark Jones was the other culprit, handling on the ground at a tackle.

It was then that Wales launched their storm and for seven minutes the Scots' 10-3 lead was severely battered. The Scottish team, however, had a highly tuned defensive awareness and it helped, of course, that the scrummage was not the sound base that the Welsh needed. Even a scrum-half with the quality, pace and vision of Robert Jones, the Welsh captain, could not construct a game without materials. He was handicapped too by the insistence of Kevin Phillips in usurping the captain's authority in decisions whether to kick or run penalties. Phillips, accustomed to taking quick penalties for Neath, had justification to keep the game flowing but such disagreements between captain and hooker could only have unsettled what composure Wales had left.

Wales, though thwarted before the interval, were not to be denied in the second half, with Phillips proving his point by exploiting a free kick to ignite the thrust for the home team's try. Robert Jones carried on to release Thorburn up the right touch-line and, when the full-back was stopped, the scrum-half slipped the ball away behind his back to spread the attack across the field for Bateman to send Arthur Emyr over on the left. Thorburn converted from well out, a goal that cut the Scots lead to 10-9 only seven minutes after the interval.

Wales immediately lost David Evans with damaged neck ligaments and, as soon

44

JIM TELFER IN COMBATIVE POSE . . . A SHOT FROM THE 1983 LIONS TOUR

as Tony Clement arrived as replacement stand-off, the Scots fired a furious assault with a series of five scrums on the home goal-line. Twice Sole opted for scrums instead of penalty kicks, an indictment of the Welsh weakness.

White was denied two scrummage pick-ups, Armstrong was squeezed into touch in the left corner and, when White varied his tactic, releasing the Scottish half-backs, Bateman conceded a penalty with a deliberate knock-on. Chalmers kicked the goal for 13-9, the score that remained for the final 22 minutes.

Scotland deserved a better margin and so it would have been had not Rene Hourquet, the French referee, twice overlooked or missed Welsh indiscipline that merited severe punishment. The first would have denied the Welsh their try, excellent score though it was in execution, and the second ought to have been punished with a penalty try.

In the lead-up to the Welsh try, just as the thrust was swinging left away from the frontal assault, Davies blatantly took Lineen out and at least twice Pugh collapsed close-range scrums immediately before the third Chalmers penalty goal. Had Hourquet reacted as he ought to have done on both occasions, the margin could have stretched by nine points.

Ignoring those infringements, if he saw them, was the way Hourquet opted out of much of his responsibility. He left the lineout mainly to take care of itself, an omission which thankfully did not spark a potential flashpoint. His was a poor performance for an international referee and it was just as well that Monsieur Hourquet's 'holiday' did not affect the result.

Scotland, though, would not blame the referee for their failure to exploit their scrummage command. Their own game outside the set piece was nervy. Sole summed up the attitude by explaining that he was concerned that a fast game might turn into a loose one that would favour the Welsh and to avoid that the Scots had to keep their rugby tighter than they might have wished.

Yet, quite apart from Cronin's try, Scotland had moments to savour, notably with sorties by Scott Hastings and Chalmers when further scores were not far away. The former's blistering pace might just have carried him over had he not slipped, and the stand-off's venture round the front of a dispersing lineout and his kick ahead all but produced a scoring finale.

In 1984 Scotland had ridden into the final match against France on the crest of the Triple Crown. Successive wins over Wales, England and Ireland had whetted the appetite but the build-up to the 1990 finale had been different. The Cardiff result — perhaps also the manner of it — was a step up the path rather than a peak itself, which the 1984 win in Dublin had been.

On the morning after the Cardiff match the Scottish squad flew home without the euphoria that had flowed from the 1984 Triple Crown match. The mood at Sunday breakfast was more akin to what it had been within the Lions' camp after the Brisbane victory in July the previous year, the result that squared the series with the deciding third Test to follow in Sydney. The Scots, like the Lions after Ballymore, had not only the satisfaction of a job well done but also the awareness of another test to follow. Ian McGeechan was a common denominator as coach of the Lions and Scotland, and eight of the Scottish XV had had the benefit of that Australian experience. He was content with the Cardiff result, even though the margin was less than it ought to have been. 'You've got to be pleased to win in Cardiff,' he claimed as one who was on the losing side in all three of his internationals there. Scotland, indeed, have won only eight times there in 95 years, though three of those have been in the past five visits — 1982, 1984, and 1990. Despite the scrummage authority, David Sole described the most recent of these as 'abrasive, as hard a game as I've had at Cardiff'. It was third time lucky for him after defeats in Cardiff in 1986 and 1988. Like the coach, the captain was satisfied with the result and so were the team. 'There's sheer delight in the dressing-room,' he said at the post-match Press conference, 'because they know how hard it is to win on this ground.' After all, only Derek White of this Scottish XV had known victory in Cardiff.

17 March 1990 at Murrayfield

SCOTLAND 13	ENGLAND 7
A. G. Hastings (*London Scottish*)	D. D. Hodgkinson (*Nottingham*)
A. G. Stanger (*Hawick*)	S. J. Halliday (*Bath*)
S. Hastings (*Watsonians*)	W. D. C. Carling (*Harlequins*) captain
S. R. P. Lineen (*Boroughmuir*)	J. C. Guscott (*Bath*)
I. Tukalo (*Selkirk*)	R. Underwood (*Leicester and RAF*)
C. M. Chalmers (*Melrose*)	C. R. Andrews (*Wasps*)
G. Armstrong (*Jed-Forest*)	R. J. Hill (*Bath*)
D. M. B. Sole (*Edinburgh Academicals*) captain	P. A. G. Rendall (*Wasps*)
K. S. Milne (*Heriot's FP*)	B. C. Moore (*Nottingham*)
A. P. Burnell (*London Scottish*)	J. A. Probyn (*Wasps*)
C. A. Gray (*Nottingham*)	P. J. Ackford (*Harlequins*)
D. F. Cronin (*Bath*)	W. A. Dooley (*Preston Grasshoppers*)
J. Jeffrey (*Kelso*)	M. G. Skinner (*Harlequins*)
D. B. White (*London Scottish*)	M. C. Teague (*Gloucester*)
F. Calder (*Stewart's-Melville FP*)	P. J. Winterbottom (*Harlequins*)

Replacement:
D. J. Turnbull (*Hawick*)
for White (28 minutes)

Replacement:
M. D. Bailey (*Wasps*)
for Guscott (65 minutes)

Try:
Stanger

Try:
Guscott

Penalty goals:
Chalmers (3)

Penalty goal:
Hodgkinson

Referee: D. J. Bishop (*New Zealand*)
Touch judges: L. J. Peard (*Wales*), W. D. Bevan (*Wales*)

48

TONY STANGER'S try immediately after the interval was timely in the 'winner-take-all' match. It was not the belated turning point that Jim Calder's try had been in the 1984 Grand Slam decider against France but the Hawick wing's score was just as crucial when added to the penalty goal that the other 21-year-old, Craig Chalmers, kicked just before half-time. The two scores stretched Scotland's tenuous 6-4 lead and the seven points that accrued were as valuable in a tight, tense contest as a dozen or more in many another game.

Afterwards, Geoff Cooke, England's team manager, placed those scores precisely in perspective. England, he remarked, could have settled for a two-point deficit at half-time. Even 4-9 would have been acceptable but to fall nine points in arrears so soon after the restart was a killer just when England should have been looking to capitalise on the wind which, though blustery and gusting, was in their favour in the second half.

Those two Scottish scores were the contest's bold features. The game's canvas, however, was coloured by fierce commitment, matching the 1987 World Cup final, when New Zealand beat France. The All Blacks that day, like Scotland against England, were convinced they knew how to play the game on their own terms against highly respected opponents. The difference was that the winners in 1987 had been pre-match favourites, though more narrowly than the bookmakers had made England.

David Sole later confirmed that the game was faster and more intense than any he had experienced. The marvel was that Scotland could keep their impetus going for the full 80 minutes. As Sole remarked, the Scots were the more 'hungry' for the quadruple grail. His masterstroke of leading them out in a single-file march, a ploy he later joked was to conserve energy, threw down the gauntlet. In the first few minutes, too, the Scots obviously wanted to take the game to the opposition, utilise the wind and impose themselves where they were strong. Finlay Calder was the spearhead in the initial assault. Driving rucks and mauls, the home forwards stated their case and they enticed the English to lose their cool.

Three times England conceded first-half penalties through indiscipline. A punch and a kick cost six points. Roger Uttley, England's coach, admitted that to concede such penalties was 'horrendous'. A word out of place after an offside penalty could have been just as costly. The extra ten metres took the Scots within range. Craig Chalmers missed that one but he was on target from 30 metres, well out to the right when the English were offside after Calder had led the charge from a tapped free kick. Four minutes into the game England were behind for the first time in this championship.

Chalmers kicked two more penalty goals, one from simple range, the other from 40 metres and again well to the right. Jeff Probyn was the first culprit, stamping on David Sole at a scrum that had fallen in, an offence signalled from the touch-line by Derek Bevan, and a punch by Paul Ackford on Chris Gray allowed Chalmers to extend the Scots' lead to 9-4 with barely five minutes of the first half left.

While edging to 6-0 the Scots had proved themselves secure at close quarters.

The stopping and chopping by Gary Armstrong and the breakaway forwards, Calder, Derek White and John Jeffrey were established qualities. Armstrong was outstanding also in covering back in defence, as he had been throughout the campaign, and Chalmers was just as safe in knocking bigger men down.

One slight chink, however, appeared in the armoury. The space four or five metres wide of the scrum was not so well policed, especially with Richard Hill feeding off Mike Teague's scrummage pick-ups. That concern appeared to weigh too heavily on the minds when Jeffrey and White detached from a scrum to cover the blind side just inside the Scottish half on the right. Chalmers drifted the same way, shadowing Rob Andrew, but Teague broke to the other side and, though Calder nabbed the English No 8, the gain line had been breached. The English forwards drove over the tackle to provide a swift ruck possession and a 4-2 overlap was created for Will Carling to send Jeremy Guscott away on a smooth run-in. The Bath centre beat Gavin Hastings with a deft dummy and England had cut back to 6-4 in 15 minutes. Simon Hodgkinson missed the conversion from the left.

Scotland, noting the ground rules, tightened up. They scrummaged on their own terms, they messed up the English lineout so effectively that much of the touch-line possession was scrappy prey for the Scots' sharper reactions, and they allowed little to escape in defence. Never again did England contrive an opening such as that made for Guscott to score. Even when, late on, Carling slipped through a couple of tackles, he was grabbed by the third wave and, the way Scotland were playing by then, it seemed a fourth and fifth would have materialised if necessary. Such thrusts by England's captain were like running through a minefield: the attacker would go only so far before, inevitably, he was blown away.

Scotland's lineout was a credit to planning. Set formats were tossed aside: White would pop up at No 2 (before his injury departure); Damian Cronin would appear at the back; Sole jumped to take one at the front. Such manoeuvrings served readily to upset the English alignment, especially on the Scottish throw-in.

Quickly taken tapped penalties also unsettled the English. By contrast, Carling at times had to convene a meeting with Hodgkinson and Brian Moore before deciding what to do with a penalty — go for goal or run it. Four times in the first half England elected not to kick for goal. Twice they opted for scrums instead of penalty kicks close to the Scottish goal-line, but to no avail.

Hodgkinson appeared to decline attempting to kick goals from two, and Carling later explained that those had been too far wide for the full-back to hope to score. Had he missed, a Scottish boot would have cleared the ball downfield and raised the siege. It was an understandable fear, though for international rugby it displayed an incredible lack of confidence in their ability to maintain pressure, if not to kick a goal.

Afterwards Uttley, though denying criticism of the referee, suggested that the Scottish scrummage was too low. Collapsed scrums were the Scots' fault, he hinted, and at least one, others claimed, ought to have cost a penalty try. Scotland, the English also claimed, were adept at killing the ball on the ground. That, though, is not the Scottish method and McGeechan retorted that New Zealand referees, such as David Bishop, 'like clear ball. They don't like bodies on the ground.' Without actually saying as much, the Scottish coach suggested that the fault in playing the ball and man on the ground was a sin more English than Scottish.

No one north of the Border could deny that Scotland played to limits the referee allowed. Bishop himself would have expected that of any good team and throughout the first quarter the Scots did not concede one penalty. It was a statistic that spoke volumes for discipline. So ordered was the Scottish game that when they lost White with a knee injury they assimilated Derek Turnbull so easily that the change, even with Jeffrey switching to No 8, was hardly noticeable. Forward planning allowed that smooth changeover: as McGeechan later remarked in a more general context, big games are won by doing the little things well.

White was injured in helping to stifle Simon Halliday on a thrust to the right corner and there followed a phase of severe pressure in which England ignored their goal-kicking opportunities. Once that assault had been repulsed, Chalmers kicked his third penalty goal.

However, when Gavin Hastings struck the second-half kick-off directly into touch allowing an England put-in at the halfway scrummage, the pressure now seemed to be back on Scotland. But the home pack found enough of a nudge to force Teague to knock on in the pick-up and, by contrast, Jeffrey's clean lift from the scrum-base released Armstrong, who found Gavin Hastings with an off-the-cuff overhead pass. The full-back juggled the ball before securing it and hoisting a kick to the right corner. Tony Stanger chased and, however fractionally, he outpaced the highly reputed wing, Rory Underwood. With a kind bounce, the Hawick youngster reached up two-handed to bring the ball down to score. The attempted conversion by Chalmers drifted wide on the wind to the far side. Rob Andrew countered with a typical, finely judged, long kick to the left corner and from a scrum there Hill attempted to put Carling over at the end of a long, flat pass. It was, though, the way by which Gavin Hastings had scored for Scotland against Fiji in October and England were surely naïve to think that the Scots would have so soon forgotten one of their own successful ploys.

A Hodgkinson penalty goal pulled the Scots' lead back to six points in the 54th minute. The full-back, however, missed two others and England were deprived when that talented centre, Guscott, had to retire with a strained hip.

By then the confidence, if not the game, was flowing in Scotland's favour. Their pack continued to work as a blanket whereas the older English forwards were looking ragged. Scott Hastings typified resilience in defence when he caught Underwood from behind, truly a try-saving tackle, and the unquenchable spirit could be seen in the break-out that Armstrong initiated by spoiling Hill at the scrum base. The Scottish forwards drove on, Calder founded a productive ruck and Armstrong wrung out 25 metres more gain with one of his grub kicks to thread the eye of a needle.

Such a counter from the home goal-line was a clear statement that the Scots had a firm grasp on the Calcutta Cup, the Triple Crown, the Five Nations' Championship and the Grand Slam. It was a grip that would not be broken.

FINAL TABLE

	P	W	D	L	F	A	Pts
Scotland	4	4	0	0	60	26	8
England	4	3	0	1	90	26	6
France	4	2	0	2	67	78	4
Ireland	3	0	0	3	22	67	0
Wales	3	0	0	3	34	76	0

Chapter Two

ABSOLUTELY NO SICK PARROTS

By DEREK DOUGLAS

ABSOLUTELY NO SICK
PARROTS

QUOTATIONS ARE THE BUILDING BLOCKS of the journalistic trade. Scribes trade them and covet them as the precious raw materials from which the sparkling columns of newspaper prose are constructed. The variety of quote to be found on the sports pages of a newspaper is generally of a different order to those inhabiting, for instance, the parliamentary pages. Some of the language to be found is most definitely of the unparliamentary variety. Not better or worse, just different. Football managers can generally be relied upon to do the business or get a result in this regard.

The quality of words spoken before, during and after Scotland's 1990 Grand Slam is, of course, of a much higher order. What follows is an extract from the hundreds of thousands of words uttered by the main protagonists. And never fear. There's not a sick parrot in sight.

We knew that we would be up against it and that the English would pose a very serious threat. The lads rose to the challenge, every single one of them, and I'm a proud man tonight. We knew it would be a battle but we just kept our heads and played our hearts out. That slow walk on to the pitch was my idea and it was meant to say that Scotland were there to win the Grand Slam too. It seemed to have the desired effect.
Scotland skipper, David Sole

This victory was no fluke. England came under an intensity of pressure they have not met before. Our nerve was stronger in front of an astonishing crowd. They were worth three points to us. I'm only worried that the All Blacks will take us quite seriously now . . .
Scotland coach, Ian McGeechan

I'm very pleased.
Assistant coach and architect of the 1984 Grand Slam, Jim Telfer. Not a man to over-egg the pudding!

There were some people, particularly in the South, who had written us off before the match even started but we always felt we could do it.
Triple penalty-kicker, Craig Chalmers

It's magnificent. It's as if the whole of Scotland was behind us today.
Scotland full-back, Gavin Hastings

Now I know what it feels like to be gutted. Up until now I had always thought it was a football euphemism.
England coach, Roger Uttley

With the benefit of hindsight we should have given Simon Hodgkinson the chance to kick when we were awarded the penalties on the Scots' line. It's easy to say that now but at the time our forwards felt they were in a strong position.
Uttley again

We want to play our own positive game unhindered by the opposition, the conditions and the referee and we are getting somewhere near that. Also, if the referee makes sure that both sides know where the offside line is that will help the game from the point of view of the spectators.
England manager, Geoff Cooke, on the eve of the match

We've had a good season. We've lost a game that's all. A truly great side has to be able to overcome the four elements — venue, weather, opposition and referee. We didn't do that today.
Cooke, speaking through clenched teeth after the match

The referee just said he wanted the scrums to stay up and after that we did our best to hold them up.
Cooke again — no loss he to the Diplomatic Corps

Scottish scavengers.
Cooke yet again, *c* 1989, as Scotland held England to a 12-12 draw at Twickenham

It's time to eat humble pie and raise one's hat.
Former England and New Zealand centre, Jaimie Salmon, now a *Daily Telegraph* rugby columnist

I'm very proud. Really chuffed.
Finlay Calder, in a TV interview moments after leaving the pitch

The English soaked up too much of the hype that always surrounds an England team. We just let them get on with thinking they would win.
Scotland flanker, John Jeffrey

WHAT A STATE! IWAN TUKALO UNDERGOES SOME OF THE FITNESS TESTING WHICH HAS HELPED HONE THE SCOTLAND
SQUAD TO PEAK PHYSICAL CONDITION

The try was as much a credit to Gavin Hastings as to me. It was a beautiful kick ahead by him and I was just lucky to be able to latch on to it.
Scotland try-scorer, Tony Stanger

Last season when we went to Wales for the championship we simply failed to play our own game. That will not happen this time. There is a different attitude. The team is crucially different and we have been much more thorough in our analysis of what we want to do and what Scotland can do.
England captain, Will Carling, on the eve of the game

We were never allowed to control the game. Scotland were the better side. We were beaten fair and square. They prepared for us and went out and beat us. Good luck to them. That's it.
Carling, after the game

It's Ian McGeechan's 50th birthday.
Nigel Starmer-Smith, underlining the perils of live television as the victorious Scottish team burst into a post-match dressing-room rendition of 'Happy Birthday' for assistant coach, Jim Telfer

Ready to take your punishment now?
Starmer-Smith again, to Scottish colleagues in the Murrayfield Press box before the game

No, we didn't wind them up too much in the dressing-room. We wanted them to think about the game. Not go through doors without opening them.
Ian McGeechan again, on BBC TV's *Wogan* show two days after the Calcutta Cup victory

Ian is the backs' coach. Maybe we had different ideas among the forwards!!
John Jeffrey, on the same show

Can I have two please? One for each ear.
English woman in East stand as she is offered a wine-gum by the wife of an over-excited and extremely voluble Scotsman

I was at Murrayfield. It was a great match and very entertaining.
Princess Anne, the Princess Royal, as she presented the awards at the BAFTA ceremony in London the day after the Grand Slam match. Son Peter was given David Sole's jersey after the match and, as patron of the SRU, she even wore her tartan scarf to the glittering awards ceremony!

England threw it away. If you can plan chaos then Ian McGeechan's plan worked perfectly. The Scots reduced England to a shambles at the end.
Ex-Wales international, Eddie Butler

I'm hurt!
England lock, Wade Dooley, as he warned friend and foe that he thought his neck had been broken

SPORTING SOME UNUSUAL HEAD-GEAR, THE RESULT OF AN EARLIER KNOCK, GARY ARMSTRONG IN ACTION AGAINST GALA AT RIVERSIDE PARK

SEAN LINEEN, THE SON OF AN ALL BLACK BUT WITH SCOTTISH BLOOD IN HIS VEINS, BROUGHT NEW PENETRATION TO THE SCOTLAND PLAY

I was scared witless. But then the daft sod started playing again.
Mrs Sharon Dooley's reaction as she saw her better half recover just as she was en route to the England dressing-room

. . . and sent him homeward tae sink again.
The Independent on Sunday displaying an inability to come to terms with the Scottish pronunciation of the climactic line in 'Flower of Scotland'. Or perhaps they did indeed get it right!

I was so choked with emotion I couldn't get the first line out. It was an incredible experience.
Ronnie Browne of The Corries, who was in the West stand for the match. Partner Roy Williamson, who wrote 'Flower of Scotland', couldn't be there because of a serious illness

If they were Masters of the Universe what does that make us?
A tired and emotional Scottish fan to nobody in particular as he stood on the Murrayfield turf just after the final whistle

The Scots (among other sterling qualities) were far better at playing the referee . . . There are those who will say Scots have always done so. As long ago as 1314 they lured poor Edward II to disaster at Bannockburn by digging the pits for his forwards to fall into . . . Scoring tries is what the game is all about. The laws should be changed to encourage open rugby . . . Today one should therefore congratulate the Scots. Nothing should be said to diminish their season's triumph. But tomorrow one should re-examine rugby — to ensure that the game retains its sporting glory.
Extract from a leading article in the august columns of *The Times* of London

JJ was up once or twice during the night but I managed to sleep.
Craig Chalmers, on the nocturnal habits of room-mate, John Jeffrey, the night before the Calcutta Cup match

The big England front five are beginning to dominate proceedings. With the wind behind them in the second half we'll be looking at a different game.
Ex-England Grand Slam skipper, Bill Beaumont, on BBC TV. So true, Bill, so true

Scotland did deserve their success. They played the game at a lot of pace. They played the referee very well as well. But their scrummage was under a lot of pressure. They collapsed it but they got away with it and good luck to them.
Beaumont again

And they WILL be celebrating down at Mansfield Park in my home town of Hawick after that great try.
Bill McLaren, poking a gentle bit of fun at himself as his former pupil, Tony Stanger, touches down for Scotland's magnificent try

I was close to tears at the finish. Finlay Calder saw how upset I was and put his arm around my shoulders to console me. I really appreciated that.
The combative England pack-leader, Brian Moore, a colleague of Calder's on the victorious 1989 tour to Australia, on how his ex-Lions skipper had extended the hand of friendship at the moment of Scotland's triumph

HAWICK SCRUM-HALF, GREIG OLIVER, ON THE BENCH THROUGHOUT THE GRAND SLAM CAMPAIGN, IN LAST SEASON'S INTERNATIONAL TRIAL

DAVID SOLE, THE WORLD-CLASS PROP WITH CRICKETERS' HANDS

Chapter Three

FAITH, HEAD, HEART . . . AND SOLE

A Tactical Appreciation

By BILL McLAREN

FAITH, HEAD AND HEART
. . . AND SOLE

ONE OF THE CRUCIAL FACTORS contributing to Scotland's Grand Slam that hasn't been accorded due credit has surely been the wisdom of appointing four coaches towards the preparation of the Scotland squad for the World Cup. That has proved of inestimable value to Scotland's fortunes for, not only are Ian McGeechan and Jim Telfer jointly renowned as top of the coaching spectrum, each having directed a Lions tour, but Derrick Grant represents magnificent back-up, as does Douglas Morgan with his vast experience as player, Scottish captain and club coach.

The pooling of ideas from those four top men has given Scotland a full head start for, not only are they men of strong views and wisdom with immensely valuable input to Scottish deliberations prior to each big game but, with two backs and two forwards in the quartet, detailed analysis of every area of play by Scotland and their opponents can be provided towards moulding the tactical influence for every game. The fact is that no senior coach, no matter how conscientious or observant, can possibly cover every area of the game. He has so much on his plate including video watching, squad session planning and implementation, individual and collective coaching, motivation, team-talks, media demands and the like; a wise senior coach can delegate duties to his assistant coaches under the Scottish system where all four are on the same wavelength.

The value of this was to be found in the task given to Derrick Grant at the Irish game — to study in detail the deployment and use of strategy at the lineouts by both countries. His treatise that followed brought about a remarkable transformation in Scotland's lineout approach, to such an extent that their lineout was transformed from something of a liability to an area of immense strength and productivity, culminating in a revolutionary pattern that was arguably the key issue in their defeat of England.

Scotland's lineout play against Ireland was disappointingly unproductive. Of

65

course the Irish are renowned lineout street fighters who stand on little ceremony and who generally have their ears to the ground insofar as assessing their referee of the day. Grant, therefore, had a lot to assess in Dublin. Apparently one of the weaknesses that struck him was that Scotland's props were not quite fulfilling their function, tending to be ball-watchers instead of minders so that the protection and support offered to Scotland's jumpers wasn't nearly aggressive enough. It was with the Lions in New Zealand in 1966 that British players, including Grant, first came across New Zealand compression at the throw-in. Each player took a step inwards and across so that they closed formation in a solid phalanx, thus ensuring that their jumper would compete on his own terms and without too much interference. England made good use of this method against Scotland two years ago and, after the English defeat of the Australians at Twickenham in November 1988, some Wallabies were a bit peeved about the manner in which England had elbowed, pushed, nudged and climbed. The Irish underlined, again to the detriment of the Scots, just how crafty and aggressive they can be in making the most of what they have in personnel and pugnacity so that, throughout the game, the Scots played second fiddle at the lineouts and struggled to win as a result. My own view also was that Damian Cronin, especially, could have used his vast bulk more effectively in contesting the jump and to offset Irish shove and lean. He may have suffered a bit from the absence of Iain Milne whose commanding presence and expertise has eased the path of sundry mid-line jumpers at every level of the game. There has also been a change in refereeing attitude. Clive Norling of Wales used to be very strict on lineout malpractice; indeed Scotland had been virtually penalised out of the Triple Crown match in Dublin in 1982. Norling, however, has now adopted a style more in accord with that of the Southern Hemisphere and French officials. Indeed it seems to me that this is something of a general trend with British referees and there seems no doubt that it was through coming to terms with this change and making adjustments on the basis of Grant's finding that Scotland enhanced their prospects. Their lineout phase then became geared to ensuring that their jumpers would not be put at a disadvantage by refereeing leniency for opposition illegality. It therefore included compression and a more belligerent style from the support players aimed at preventing their opposite numbers from putting pressure on Scotland's jumpers who then were placed in a more favourable situation as one against one or, on some occasions, one against none! There was, too, the subtle use of Derek White near the front as an additional threat in a somewhat unorthodox role, a form of unexpected switch in positioning that was to be extended to quite startling effect in the Grand Slam decider against England. Thus, no other jumpers in the championship, except perhaps England's Wade Dooley, gained the same ascendancy over the Scots as that achieved by Ireland's Donal Lenihan, Willie Anderson and Noel Mannion who, it has to be said, had already given the All Blacks heave-ho.

Scotland's concern over their misfortunes in the Dublin lineouts were well founded. Shortage of lineout ball placed a heavy strain on the Scottish scrummage

CHUFFED...IWAN TUKALO CELEBRATES A 1988 TRY AGAINST THE IRISH

which, happily, throughout the championship grew stronger and more reliable as David Sole took lowering pressure in his stride and Paul Burnell emerged from the shadow of Iain Milne with scrummage surety to set alongside his mobility and splendid tackling. There was the point, too, that whenever Scotland did win a lineout ball in Dublin, they made profit from it as, for instance, when a clean take by Chris Gray — and he made a number of those in the championship — sparked a thrilling drive from which the most positive handling attack was launched involving four Scottish forwards and two backs. It should have spawned a try.

The problem with the French lineout is in stopping them getting beyond the gain-line two or three times prior to feeding their backs, with part of Scotland's midfield defence sucked in. With their scrum-half throwing in, the French invariably drive their lineout through a front-row forward in the scrum-half position and then create further thrusts through loose forwards standing off. Their midfield then tends to thrive on the ball being speedily whipped to them by that clever master of continuity, scrum-half Pierre Berbizier, in whose footsteps Henri Sanz has followed as to the manner born. It had to be part of Scotland's plan to check the French before they breached the gain-line so that they might be forced to move the ball to their backs before any of Scotland's midfield had been drawn out of position. The Scots were eminently successful in this because of the quite marvellous tackling, especially by their three loose forwards, John Jeffrey, Derek White and Finlay Calder, with Cronin setting the tight forwards a splendid example to which they responded with total commitment and vigour. It has also been a mighty plus for Scotland that they have two additional flanker-type tacklers in Gary Armstrong and Craig Chalmers, each being prepared to engage anyone of any size showing his face up the fringe or in a standing-off role. On a one-to-one basis, too, Scotland's centres, Scott Hastings and Sean Lineen, have generally been impregnable so that there was nothing like the threat from France's midfield that there had been in previous seasons.

The Scots had also done their homework on Welsh set-piece play before going to Cardiff and it resulted in one of their most satisfying successes of the campaign. They knew from videos that when Neath throw long to Mark Jones, the first link man is usually Brian Williams using a flying start from the front lineout position. So, as soon as Scotland won a long Welsh throw, Gary Armstrong, as planned, attacked the front which was comparatively uninhabited. The plan included immediate support from John Jeffrey and David Sole and, although Sole's pass was too awkward for Ken Milne, Cronin charged up, again according to plan, to register Scotland's only try. It was another masterly piece of preparation that bore fruit, as indeed did Scotland's almost total neglect of Chris Gray as a front jumper so as to virtually play the powerful Phil Davies out of the lineout game.

The physical change in Scotland's lineout approach was most evident against Wales. The match was refereed by France's Rene Hourquet and his lineout style usually involves allowing the participants to 'referee' the lineouts unless some knuckle is thrown. Scotland, therefore, made sure that they would not be placed

68

at a disadvantage by exploiting Hourquet's method with some of the most effective compression that one has seen from Scottish forwards. They simply squeezed the Welsh out of it and this was coupled with some clever manoeuvring by Cronin, who completely outplayed the 21-year-old Gareth Llewellyn of Neath who probably learned more about the fruity bits of lineout application in one afternoon than in the rest of his career.

One other great success of Scotland's coaching partnership, and especially of Jim Telfer, is that they have transformed a moderate front five into one that is unlikely to give ground to anyone, even the All Blacks. Admittedly this has been one of the weakest Welsh sides for years, lacking hwyl, tackle and pattern but the side that played Scotland was stronger than that annihilated by England. Even so, Scotland's tight five gave one of the most productive displays by any Scottish front five since the days of Ian McLauchlan, Quintin Dunlop or Duncan Madsen, Sandy Carmichael, Gordon Brown and Alistair McHarg in the early 1970s. Their intelligence had told them that the Welsh lacked ballast in their front row so they attacked them there and found, as they had suspected, that they could hold the Welsh scrummage with only seven forwards. Thus, when the Welsh created several scrummages near Scotland's goal-line, Jeffrey was able to detach and was lying in wait for the pick-up drive that they knew Mark Jones would attempt up Scotland's left side. With aid from a quick-breaking White, Jeffrey stifled that threat every time. The Welsh played into Scotland's hands by their predictability. Had Mark Jones, as a variant, served a wide-breaking Robert Jones on the other side, Scotland might have had more trouble. As it was they had none at all. In any event, Robert Jones would have had to be very sharp to escape the Jed-Forest mongoose, Armstrong, with back-up from Calder.

Arguably the most rewarding tactical success by the Scots was at the lineout in the deciding game against England. Not only did it lessen the menace of one of the strongest areas of the English game but it created a situation of immense pleasure to thousands of Scots — that of big English forwards being unsure of exactly what was happening on the touch-line and, indeed, what to do about it. The Scots obviously reasoned that, in orthodox-type lineouts, they would be at a disadvantage against two such big and acknowledged specialists as Wade Dooley and Paul Ackford, not to mention two of the most astute and ruthless jungle protectors, Paul Rendall and Mike Teague. Two years previously, virtually the same Englishmen had wrecked Scotland's lineout and, during the 1990 championship, they had exerted almost total control of the lineout play after surviving their hardest toil at Ireland's hands. Scotland sought to destroy that element of lineout control and their method of doing so was cleverly conceived and brilliantly executed. It reminded older rugby men of the pre-war years when virtually every forward in the lineout was a jumper and the ball might be thrown to anyone of them. It entailed the Scottish forwards continually switching positions so that almost no line was the same as the previous one. The loose forwards frequently appeared at the front, Calder once making a lovely catch at number one, Cronin drifting between four, five and six and Derek Turnbull

DEREK TURNBULL...THE HAWICK FLANKER'S ABILITY TO KNOCK MEN BACK IN THE TACKLE HAS BEEN A MAJOR FACTOR IN HIS EMERGENCE ON THE INTERNATIONAL SCENE

between two, three and five. It caused confusion in English ranks and puzzled expressions on faces as when, for instance, Ackford suddenly found he was marking Jeffrey one minute and Turnbull the next. The appearance of Turnbull also underlined how astute has been Scotland's choice of back-up men, for the blond Hawick captain, never less than abrasive, revelled in the physical confrontation and certainly helped to lessen the effect of Rendall and Teague as spoilers of opposing jumpers. The Scots thus gave themselves room and the chance to live on their wits and although they still couldn't stop Dooley from turning back some good ball, they certainly denied England the rich platform they had enjoyed in previous games.

It stressed again the advance made by Scotland's tight five that, even against a mighty and heavier England scrummage that had rolled the Welsh backwards like an earth-remover at work, the Scottish scrummage, hinges squeaking a bit early on, dug in and even denied the English the close-range try that seemed on the cards. Of course there was controversy afterwards over whether Scotland should have been penalised for taking down the scrummages, as happened three times, and whether England shouldn't once have been given a penalty try. David Sole has been around for quite some time and no one probably has more worldly wisdom of what goes on in the darkened recesses of the front row. At one time he made no bones about it. If his opposite number was pulling him down he just went down, got up ready to start again, hopeful 'that the referee was on your side'. Of course, props will take the scrummage down as a last resort to prevent a push-over score against them, but at the same time they do risk conceding a penalty try. Scotland's scrummage had been squeezed but not driven and Jeff Probyn is a very disruptive scrummager in either lowering or boring in on the rival hooker. One Englishman suggested that Probyn would never take a scrummage down five metres from the opponents' line. Wouldn't he? It might bring a penalty try if the referee read it wrong. It is an area that always will raise controversy because it is so hard to apportion blame fairly. That scrummage performance against England in particular must have given Paul Burnell immense satisfaction. He may not quite be the pressurising bulwark that is Iain Milne but he established himself as an integral part of a Scottish pack that learned so much from the opening test against Ireland and never then looked back.

Perhaps the one disappointing aspect of Scottish strategy was that so little effort was made to reach out for more expansive style. Scotland scored only six tries and conceded three in the four championship games. Only two of their tries were scored by backs — England scored 12, of which ten were by backs, France, nine and eight by backs. Scotland seldom hinted at the kind of ball transference among the backs that England achieved as the most attractive side in the campaign. England, of course, produced a shoal of slot-machine deliveries but the main reason for their ability to spin them wide was the possession of two half-backs who had the vision and technique to ship it quick and provide line handling when the chance was on. Richard Hill had the quickest hands in the championship although no quicker, one hastened to inform him, than those of Ewan McCorkindale of

GARY ARMSTRONG HAS GOT IT TAPED... THE SCOTLAND SCRUM-HALF REVIEWS THE HISTORIC CALCUTTA CUP MATCH ON TV

IWAN TUKALO...A DEVASTATING FINISHER AND ALWAYS A PROLIFIC TRY-SCORER

Glasgow High-Kelvinside. For all his many admirable qualities Gary Armstrong is a fraction slower in service. Rob Andrew has developed into a complete stand-off for he is quick, he punts with precision and, most important, he is a shrewd judge of the difference between the bad ball and quality ball. One you hoof or give back to forwards for a brush and polish, the other you use for threat or launch, and the quicker the launch the better for those outside. That is an area of Craig Chalmers's game that will be honed with more experience and practice.

Scotland's strategy comprised using the boot to create pressure situations and using their pivot five as a means of keeping the ball within reach of their forwards. They also made fruitful use of the narrow side, as when Armstrong brilliantly launched that Tony Stanger try against England and earlier there had been slick handling for that amazing try by Iwan Tukalo against France when he stuttered, fell, got up and, by sheer refusal to be stopped, gave Scotland a clinching cushion. Another feature was the use made of Gavin Hastings as a narrow-side intruder as when he chipped ahead for Stanger's try and later almost did the same aimed on the other flank. Scotland's style aimed at eliminating risks and error, putting the pressure on opponents so as to capitalise on their mistakes and supporting that with a collective approach to the tackle that was quite wondrous to behold. Every player, from Gavin Hastings to David Sole, played his part in laying down a solid blanket that was holed in the championship only three times — by John Fitzgerald of Ireland, somewhat fortuitously up the side of a maul, by Arthur Emyr — when too many Scots were dragged left by Paul Thorburn's thrust, and super linkage by Ritchie Collins, and by Jeremy Guscott, on the only occasion that Scott Hastings was beaten man-to-man — and that more by the perfect weight and flight of Richard Hill's pass than by Will Carling's speed of foot. No side in the championship has put opponents on the floor with such consistency. Scotland's battle plans were really simple but the basic requirements were there and stopping the other lot from doing the things they wanted to do by copybook tackling was definitely high on this Scotland's agenda. So often, too, the Scots achieved that other priority of denying opponents time on the ball, engaging them so quickly as to affect their option choice adversely.

There were rare successes in other realms of planning. Seldom in his career has the gifted Serge Blanco been so embarrassed as at Murrayfield when a series of searching Chalmers punts, with thundering follow-up from Hastings, Lineen and the loose forwards, wrecked his composure and concentration. The Scots were also very much on their toes for those quick tap penalties and throw-ins, so beloved of the Neath side and which Ron Waldron, the new Welsh coach, hoped to transfer to the national side by the inclusion of seven players from the Neath club brought by him to a state of near invincibility in his own country. Homework again was Scotland's ally.

Scotland's style was based on a very fit and very mobile pack, capable of combative operations anywhere on the paddock and for the full 80 minutes, and on backs who played to their strengths and who never flinched from unglamorous forward chores when the situation demanded.

74

Also a feature of Scotland's success were the individually inspiring performances in each game of the campaign. Derek White reached a new peak against Ireland, altogether apart from his two tries — the second of which was a model of pick-up technique and speed — and acute awareness of where he was and what he could do as he dotted down one-handed and at full stretch. Craig Chalmers provided a handsome fillip with that heel-tap tackle on the flying Pierre Hontas — a try then could have changed the entire complexion of the game. John Jeffrey gave one of the most complete flanker performances one has ever been privileged to see at Cardiff — and to think that one felt that he had gone stale earlier in the season through a surfeit of rugby! And, as if to let his twin brother, Jim, know that he wasn't the only Calder who could feature in a Grand Slam, Finlay, of that ilk, was immense against England as, indeed, were Gary Armstrong, who just kept on tackling, and Gavin Hastings, who just kept on sending his forwards back upfield. And, of course, the tackle of the championship was that by Scott Hastings, who denied Rory Underwood a try that would have put him into the record books with Carston Catcheside (England), Johnny Wallace (Scotland) and Patrick Esteve and Philippe Sella (France) as the only ones to have scored a try in each of the four internationals in a championship.

But perhaps the most inspiring segment of vivid action in the entire England game was when Will Carling took a long, miss-pass flat out from Hill then took on the look of a man who had been hit by a typhoon as the entire Scottish pack got in behind the first tackler, Craig Chalmers, and shunted Carling back at a rate of knots. That surely was when the English knew that it was not to be their day.

Whilst most of Scotland's penalties were kicks to touch or at goal, it was pleasing to note their use of quick, tap penalties as part of their plan to prevent England from settling to their established routine. The English game also brought Scotland's best efforts at accepting calculated risks by a more expansive style in which Lineen has shown an astute feel for angles and lines of running — as when he created White's first try, against Ireland. However, Scotland won the Grand Slam without a single drop goal, curious when one considers the past value of John Rutherford's record of 12 successive drops and the fact that Craig Chalmers not only opened his international account with a beauty against Wales last season but slotted in seven during the Lions tour in Australia last summer.

Throughout the four games Scotland's pattern of play might have been more restricted than the coaches would have wished but their commitment was exceptional, their tackling incredible, their *esprit de coeur* unshakable. As Clive Rowlands, that legendary Welsh character and a staunch admirer of Ian McGeechan with whom he shared the Lions success in Australia, said to me on his way to the Hong Kong sevens with his Welsh International squad: 'Scotland won because they used this (pointing to his head), they had this (pointing to his heart) and because, most of all, they had faith in their plan. They were bloody great.'

It was during another Lions tour of New Zealand, in 1983, that the eight Scots realised that they were just as good players as any of the others and that they had nothing to fear from any of the Five Nations countries. That was when the seeds were sown of the confidence that took Scotland to their 1984 Grand Slam with the broad nucleus formed by that Lions representation. I believe that something similar led to this 1990 success for although the English were the ones who took most of the credit for the Lions' Test Series win and themselves benefited from the remarkable coaching talent that is Ian McGeechan, the Scots returned home with something to prove and having themselves learned a lot about their future opponents.

There is no doubt, also, that thoughtful, consistent selection has been a very important factor. Never in Scottish rugby history has the same side played throughout a championship. This one did, although Derek Turnbull brought the number to 16 when he replaced Derek White against England. Nothing builds a player's confidence quicker than the knowledge that he will be given a fair chance to establish himself in the side. The convenor of the selection commitee, Bob Munro, and the other members, Ian McGeechan, Derrick Grant, Duncan Paterson, Graham Young and Ian Lawrie, have served their time, have their feet firmly planted on the ground and realise the value of allowing players time to gel. They knew too, as John Rutherford once said, that it takes more than one season for a player to acclimatise to all the very peculiar demands of international play. They took a chance last season with Armstrong, Chalmers and Burnell. This season they invested in Tony Stanger. Such has been their care and consistency that all the backs, except Stanger, have had two full seasons of internationals together and the entire pack that started against England were together in an international for the eighth time. No wonder this Scottish side is likened to a club team in the realms of getting on really well with each other, having confidence in colleagues and having created an understanding of the plan and the repertoire and of how each player has to slot into that method. The selectors also deserve a pat on the back for their choice of David Sole as captain in the wake of Finlay Calder's successful leadership of the Lions in Australia. Calder's reaction to Sole's appointment reflected again the intense unity of purpose within the squad. Sole really did take charge and made himself responsible with hard decisions such as to switch the goal-kicking from Hastings to Craig Chalmers. Personally, I would have stuck with Hastings for he was striking the ball cleanly enough but fractionally off-target. I believe he would have kicked himself back into the wonderful form that brought him six penalty goals in his début against France in 1986. The young Chalmers has almost, but not quite, hit more drunken goals than Peter Brown but certainly he has hit the target to justify Sole's decision. Sole, too, has handled the demands of the media with good sense and patience. He has been a model captain and his decision to walk on to Murrayfield for the English game, instead of running on, was a master-stroke. It reminded me of 1935 at Mansfield Park when the huge Jack Manchester, with black scrum-cap, ball in one hand, the size of a bucket lid, marched his All Blacks on to play the South. A frightening lot they were. Sole's slow march and that inspiring rendering of 'Flower of Scotland' by the massed choir will live long in the memories of all who experienced it.

SCOTLAND STAND-OFF, CRAIG CHALMERS, AND REPLACEMENT SCRUM-HALF, GREIG OLIVER

The respect bordering on reverence that the players had for 'Geech' and 'Creamy' Telfer was arguably the most influential factor of all. McGeechan admitted to having watched videos of the France v England game three times for two hours each. He had noted how England's opponents 'couldn't get at them' and how England were 'a momentum side' where they were allowed to build on that control of their possession. All of Scotland's coaches are committed video watchers and it was a massive tribute to McGeechan, Telfer and the others that the Scottish side took the field with a clear imprint of how they wanted to play, of how they could make it hard for their opponents to strike a game and with a confidence born of superb fitness, mobility and careful preparation.

National League rugby has played its part, too, in providing a tougher programme of matches which really do matter so that players nowadays are more often subjected to genuine pressurised rugby at a pace that makes it easier to graduate to district and trials play. The number of national tours undertaken also aids the development of players. Derek Turnbull's card was marked on the demanding tour to Spain and France in 1986, Craig Chalmers played in four of the five games in Zimbabwe in 1988 where Paul Burnell also made a good impression, and Tony Stanger returned from just two of the five games in Japan in 1989 to become Scotland's Grand Slam right wing. Chalmers has demonstrated that there is a stairway to the stars for young Scots for he has graduated through Scottish Schools, all youth sections, the South, Scotland B and is now part of history as a Grand Slam stand-off.

Clubs, too, are either enhancing the work done for rugby in schools or, indeed, taking it over altogether. The success of Stirling County and Jed-Forest in creating productive youth policies stands as a model and incentive. To see 120 youngsters in action at Bridgehaugh at weekends holds out confidence for the future of the Scottish game which, despite problems in keeping interest alive in some schools, is in good heart. The choice of Scotland's party for their tour of New Zealand hinted at some youthful talent battering on the door — Stuart Porter (Malone), Craig Redpath, Graeme Shiel and George Weir (Melrose) and Shade Munro (Glasgow High-Kelvinside), all players of high promise who will reap the benefit of that experience in New Zealand which, of course, also will provide an accurate gauge of exactly where Scotland stands in world rankings.

That rating has to be pretty high with high promise of Scotland making a stronger impact on the World Cup, which is gradually creeping nearer, especially as all Scotland's early games will be at Murrayfield with 'Flower of Scotland' to stir the blood. For a wee country accustomed to long hungers of comparative failure and very short bursts of uplifting success, Scotland does wonderfully well. Murrayfield, 17 March 1990, just after four o'clock, provided ample proof of that.

Chapter Four

WHAT THE PAPERS SAID

By DEREK DOUGLAS

WHAT THE PAPERS SAID

THE GREAT MURRAYFIELD SHOOT-OUT generated unprecedented levels of media interest. In the week before the Grand Slam match, radio, television and newspapers gave the game blanket coverage. Match tickets were changing hands — it is said — for four-figure sums and the Scottish Rugby Union issued stern warnings as to the consequences for those dabbling in the black market. The Edinburgh constabulary got in on the act, too, with the threat of arrest for any touts seen operating outside the ground.

The London-based media made no secret of how they considered the result a foregone conclusion. England would win. It was hardly worth the Scots turning up. Unfortunately for England this barrage of heavyweight English propaganda was decidedly counter-productive. The more the Scots read of English superiority the more it galvanised the spirit of not just the team but the nation, or at least that part of it which takes an interest in rugby.

Scotland had decided, after the match against the Welsh in Cardiff, that the tag of underdog would do nicely, thank you. In contrast to the tone of comments coming from the England camp, those escaping the lips of Scottish coach, Ian McGeechan, and skipper, David Sole, were always along the lines of: 'Yes England are a fine side and they have played some fine rugby this season, and if we are to beat them we will have to improve on what we have done so far.'

The confidence in the England camp transmitted itself to the camp followers in the London media or was it the other way around! How about this example by the Press Association's rugby correspondent, Terry Cooper, on the eve of the game? The PA is the national news agency whose copy is taken by almost all large British newspapers. Cooper's despatch from the England pre-match camp at Peebles, which appeared under the heading, 'England approach perfection', began: 'England had a near perfect training session this morning, as they completed their preparations for tomorrow's Grand Slam shoot-out against Scotland. ''Not one ball was dropped during the hour,'' said manager, Geoff Cooke, ''and there were only a couple of minor technical faults.'' '

81

In a second piece, and positively warming to his task, Cooper, who was by no means alone in his misplaced optimism, declared: 'Will Carling's England start as red hot favourites,' and then proceeded to run a gauge over the Scotland line-up. He concluded, in essence, England has nothing to worry about. He declared:

> There is only one area where Scotland can claim superiority and decreasing evidence that England can be matched in other departments.
>
> Gavin Hastings, despite his erratic goal-kicking, is still certain to be a more influential full-back than Simon Hodgkinson but England have prevented Hodgkinson's possible defensive deficiencies being exposed . . .
>
> David Sole, Scotland's captain, is recognised as a world-class loose-head, though Rendall, in the English scrum, is more effective now than at the start of this season. '
>
> Scotland's back row of Finlay Calder, Derek White and Jeffrey, might be faster than the English trio, but they cannot match the aggressive, tough, physical presence of Mickey Skinner, Mike Teague and Peter Winterbottom.
>
> Scotland's centres, Scott Hastings and Sean Lineen, are artisans compared with the artistry of Jeremy Guscott, who was labelled the best centre on the Lions' tour last year by Ian McGeechan who now finds himself, as Scotland's coach, trying to halt the seven Englishmen whom he did so much to develop while in Australia.
>
> Guscott's centre partner, Carling, is an abrasive, creative, try-scoring midfield back.
>
> The two sectors where England will expect to control and win the match are at lock and half-back. Wade Dooley and Paul Ackford are the confirmed top alliance in winning lineout ball.
>
> Scotland are probably handicapped by the fact that their pair, Damian Cronin and Chris Gray, play in the English first division and have their weaknesses revealed to English eyes every week.
>
> England half-backs, Richard Hill and Rob Andrew, typify a phenomenon in the side. They are two of several who were disappointments in their earlier days on the international scene but who are now playing with skill and productive assurance that borders on arrogance.
>
> Because of the Lions' tour, the teams know all about each other, but the slightly unknown factor is New Zealand referee David Bishop.
>
> England manager Cooke says: 'If Mr Bishop makes sure that both sides know where the offside line is, that will help the game from the point of view of the spectators.'
>
> (Mr Cooper explains:) This is Cooke's diplomatic way of saying he wants the Scottish back row and centres to stay on-side — something to which they are seldom accustomed . . . .
>
> It will be a major surprise and a shattering disappointment to the squad if England lose.

And finally, having worked himself into a frenzy of misguided confidence, and apparently with 'Land of Hope and Glory' playing in the background, Cooper exclaims: 'It was surely symbolic that yesterday the English party trod on Scottish soil exactly ten years to the minute since the Grand Slam was completed on

15 March, 1980.' That sound you hear now, Terry, that's not 'Land of Hope and Glory'. That's the noise chickens make when they come home to roost!

Although they claim that it was not the case, the England camp would have been less than human if they had not been affected by this relentless hype. If you tell a team often enough that they are world-beaters then in large or short measure they will begin to believe it. It does seem now that the England players, coaching staff and hierarchy simply fell into the age-old trap of believing their own publicity. Sure, they felt that Scotland would give them a good game but they saw the Calcutta Cup match as simply a port of call en route to the World Cup of 1991.

The result, as they saw it, was a foregone conclusion. Bring on the All Blacks was the cry.

The great Grand Slam showdown at Murrayfield inflamed the sporting passions in a way that no game of rugby has ever done before, and probably never will again. Here is a before, during and after selection of newspaper headlines:

THURSDAY, 15 MARCH

WIN AT ALL COSTS (Rob Andrew)
SCOTTISH TERRIERS TO BEAT ODDS (Welsh wing, Arthur Emyr)
Today

ENGLAND KEEPING CALM
SOLE GIVES HEART TO THE BODY OF SCOTLAND
WOODWARD WAITS FOR TEST OF DEFENCE
INVADING ENGLISH KEEPING LOW PROFILE
The Times

SCRUMBLIES FACE A RIGHT RUCKIN'
(Welsh star Richie Collins on the England pack)
DOOLEY'S EVEN GOT VILLAINS RUNNING
The Sun

ANDREW'S JACKPOT WARNING
TAKE THE HIGH ROAD — HODGKINSON JUST NOT UP TO IT
STAND UP AND MAKE GAME FLOW, SAYS REF
Scottish Daily Express

CROWNING MOMENT FOR BISHOP
Glasgow Herald

MAN IN THE MIDDLE AT MURRAYFIELD
The Scotsman

FRIDAY, 16 MARCH

SCOTS PRESSURE MUST BE NAME OF THE GAME
ENGLAND'S LIONS ALREADY KNOW McGEECHAN'S WAY
Glasgow Herald

ENGLAND HOT FAVOURITES IN GRAND SLAM CLASSIC
Press Association

CARLING'S PLANNING TO RULE IN 1990
JEFFREY IN THE MOOD TO BATTER ENGLAND
COOKE SORRY OVER 'SCAVENGERS' SLUR
Daily Express

SCOTS RATED MOST AWKWARD OPPONENTS
COOKE SAYS REF'S CONTROL CRUCIAL
The Scotsman

THE PRESSURE IS ON BUT ENGLAND SHOULD WIN WITH EASE
(Steve Smith)
Daily Mail

SATURDAY, 17 MARCH

FINGERS CROSSED FOR A GRAND SLAM
Glasgow Herald

ENGLAND TO GRASP THE GRAND PRIZE
The Independent

GRAND SLAM DECIDER A STEPPING STONE TO WORLD CUP PRIZE
Daily Telegraph

DREAM START IS KEY TO DREAM GAME
The Times

SCOTS AIM TO SET FAST PACE
The Scotsman

SLAM 'EM. SEND ENGLAND HOME TO THINK AGAIN
Daily Record

MAYHEM THREAT AT MURRAYFIELD
Scottish Daily Express

AN OLD WARHORSE SCENTING BATTLE (on Roger Uttley)
The Guardian

SUNDAY, 18 MARCH

A GRAND SLAM FROM THE SCOTS
Observer

INEPT ENGLAND SLAMMED BY SCOTLAND
Observer Scotland

SCOTLAND'S SLAM AS ENGLAND FLOP
Sunday Times

GREAT SCOTS — ENGLAND BLOW IT
TARTAN TORTURE
Sunday Mirror

WHAT A WIN . . . WHAT A TEAM
OUR HEROES
Sunday Mail

THE FLOWER OF SCOTLAND
Scotland on Sunday

SCOTLAND THE BRAVE
Mail on Sunday

SCOTS GRAND SLAM — WITH HELP FROM OOR WULLIE
LOWER OF SCOTLAND — NOW FOR NEW ZEALAND
Sunday Post

SCOTLAND DELIVER THE GRAND FLOURISH
SOLE'S DESTROYERS CREATE CHAOS TO TURN BACK
FLAWED ENGLISH INVASION
The Sunday Correspondent

A GRAND WIN INSPIRED BY AULD ENEMY
FLOWER OF SCOTLAND
Sunday Express

SCOTLAND FIND CROWNING GLORY
TO LEAVE ENGLAND SLAMMED
The Sunday Telegraph

MURRAYFIELD GOES BARMY
SLAM BANG
SLICK SCOTS FLOOR 'EM
The People

SCOTLAND WALK TALL TO PULL OFF GLORIOUS WIN
IT'S GRAND!
News of the World

MONDAY, 19 MARCH

PURE COURAGE, HEART AND SOLE
SCOTS NOW BEST IN EUROPE
PRINCESS TURNS UP WITH TARTAN SCARF
Glasgow Herald

RAMPANT SCOTS GET IT RIGHT
The Scotsman

THE GRANDEST SLAM
SALUTE OUR FLOWER POWER!
SUPER SCOTS DESTROY 'INVINCIBLES'
Daily Record

NOW WE'LL MAUL ALL BLACKS
PRIDE FIRED US UP, ROARS SCOTT
The Sun

HOW SCOTLAND MADE A DREAM COME TRUE
Daily Mail

TOAST OF SCOTLAND
ENGLAND THROW IT ALL AWAY
Today

SOLE TRAIN ROLLS OVER ENGLAND
NOW FOR THE ALL BLACKS
Scottish Daily Express

SCOTLAND STAGE GRAND REBELLION
The Independent

ENGLISH ARMY SENT HOME TO THINK AGAIN
The Times

SCOTLAND SLAM THOSE OF LITTLE FAITH
EVEN ALL BLACKS WILL RESPECT THOSE TRIPLE CHAMPIONS
Daily Telegraph

ALL BLACKS NEXT FOR McGEECHAN'S GUERRILLAS
The Guardian

TUESDAY, 20 MARCH

CARLING WAS WRONG, SAYS UTTLEY
OUR HELL, UTTLEY'S LAMENT
Daily Mirror

SUNDAY, 25 MARCH

ENGLAND STILL THE SEASON'S GREATEST TEAM
Sunday Times

A SONG OF THE HEART
The Observer

YOU CAN BEAT THE ALL BLACKS (Andy Dalton)
News of the World

HIGH ROAD TO NEW ZEALAND LITTERED WITH POT HOLES
(Eddie Butler)
DREAMING IN A SCOTCH MIST
The Sunday Correspondent

NOW A STIFFER TEST IN STORE FOR SCOTLAND'S
MASTER PLANNER McGEECHAN
Independent on Sunday

GRAND TO BE SCOTTISH
Sunday Mail

SLAMS PAST, PRESENT . . . AND FUTURE?

By BRIAN MEEK

SLAMS PAST, PRESENT
... AND FUTURE?

AFTER SCOTLAND had beaten England 14-11 on 21 March 1925, the teams, the referee and the touch judges, plus the committees of both unions, repaired to the Freemasons' Halls in Hill Street, Edinburgh, for a bite of supper. Toasts were given to either side and one to the referee — an event which has disappeared from the modern list — and, during a jolly evening, John Bannerman, the Scottish second-row forward and factor to the Duke of Montrose, taught Gaelic songs to a couple of the English forwards, D. C. Cumming and R. R. F. MacLennan.

The Scots were absolutely delighted to have recovered the Calcutta Cup, a trophy which had eluded them since two years before the outbreak of the First World War. They were also quite pleased, although it did not mean quite as much to most, to have won the International Championship. Not one of them realised, or would even have recognised the term, that they had just completed the Grand Slam. It had never happened before and would not again for 59 long years.

There are only two of the 1925 team still alive today, 92-year-old Bob Howie, the former Kirkcaldy prop, who lives in sheltered accommodation in Denny, Loanhead, and the 86-year-old ex-Glasgow High School FP hooker, Jimmy Ireland, living alone in a flat in Polmont. It is through Ireland's bright eyes that I traced the march of the first Grand Slam.

He was 21 and working in the accountancy branch of the Singer Manufacturing Company which had, at the time, some 11,000 or so employees. The bosses were not much impressed by star rugby players, soccer was the big game in the West — and when, as an internationalist, Ireland asked for a Saturday off he was indeed queried by his superior: 'Do you really need the whole day?' For Scotland's home games he would take the 11 o'clock train from Glasgow Queen Street and meet the others for lunch at the North British Hotel. This was the 1920s equivalent of a squad session.

But Ireland was still uncapped at the start of the Grand Slam season and was summoned as a reserve for the first match against France on 24 January, the last international to be played at Inverleith, home of Daniel Stewart's FP. Ireland didn't sit on a bench as there wasn't one and would not have been called on to play if anyone had been injured after the start — replacements were decades away — but he did receive an invitation to the dinner.

There were only 20,000 spectators to see Scotland win 25-4 with Ian Smith, the Oxford wing, scoring four tries. But more of him anon. Ireland's outstanding memory is of a mighty dropped goal by the French fly-half, du Manoir.

Despite the result the Scottish selectors, meeting immediately after the game, were far from satisfied with the performance of their pack. Bannerman, even then the kind of senior pro of the side, took Ireland aside and told him he would be in the team to meet Wales. 'I didn't believe him,' says Jimmy now. The famous postcard duly arrived and Ireland, along with Howie and Doug Davies of Hawick, were the new front row to go to Swansea. They received one blue jersey, with strict instructions not to lose it, were told to bring their own boots and socks and, after the game, were presented with a cap. If you wanted to print the dates of your appearances on the famous headgear, you paid.

Swansea doubled as a cricket ground and Jimmy remembers that the railings slanted away from the touch-line which was 'rather disconcerting'. The flying Smith was far from put off; he grabbed another four tries, Scotland led 18-0 at half-time and trotted home fairly comfortably 24-14. Even if they didn't realise it, they were halfway to the Grand Slam.

So let's take an interval breather for a summary by Ireland of his team-mates.

'Dan Drysdale, the Heriot's full-back, was a player ahead of his time in that he quite often joined in the attacks. He had also played stand-off which was an asset and was a fine goal-kicker.

'Ian Smith was a most delightful man, full of mischief, who never took himself, or rugby, all that seriously. He was big, strong and so very fast that very few could contain him. Some people thought that Smith was pretty dumb, the chap who always counted on his fingers when he played pontoon. It was an act. Ian had qualified as a chartered accountant then he met a friend in Princes Street who needed a partner for a law practice. Smith went away and took a law degree.

'G. P. S. Macpherson was the other half of the partnership, a player who really knew the game. It was he who took me aside before that Swansea match and, in five minutes, I had learned more about rugby, and myself, than ever before. Phil Macpherson had pace and a wonderful side step. Frankly he didn't go around looking for people to tackle, he always said he was no use to us on the ground but he could defend when he had to.

'The other centre was G. G. Aitken, a New Zealander, and Johnny Wallace, born in Australia, was the left-wing and pretty quick too. For the first two games in 1925 the fly-half was J. C. Dykes of Glasgow Academicals. For the last two it was Herbert Waddell of Glasgow Academicals. They were a magnificent club side then, the best, perhaps, I have ever seen and they also provided the scrum-half Jimmy Nelson. He was prepared to take on the opposition single-handed; Gary

THE SCOTLAND TEAM TO FACE WALES AT SWANSEA IN 1925. THE SCOTS WON 14 - 24

THE 1984 GRAND SLAM HEROES...BEFORE THE IRISH MATCH AT LANSDOWNE ROAD

Armstrong reminds me a little of him. Herbert was my friend for more than half a century. Maybe he wasn't in the same class as some of the Welsh fly-halves but he was never afraid to try things and his tackling was superb. Davies and Howie, my props, were both farmers and enormously strong. In the second row we had Bannerman, 13½ stone at his heaviest, and Dr David MacMyn from London Scottish. John Bannerman was a remarkable man, full of enthusiasm for life. Politically he started out as a Socialist, became a Nationalist and wound up as a Liberal — he always wanted to try everything!

'Our back row was ''Jumbo'' Scott of Stewart's, Dr Sandy Gillies from Carlisle, who did a bit of goal-kicking, and ''Sealy'' Paterson of Birkenhead Park, not very big but who was everywhere.

'We played in a simple, open style, always with the idea of putting the ball out to the backs. In our day you had to play the ball with your foot after a tackle or when it had gone to ground. That meant the ball was always visible. In my opinion, when that law changed, rugby suffered as a result. I don't much like all the wrestling and mauling of the game today.'

Macpherson missed the next game, against Ireland at Lansdowne Road, and in his absence Smith was a bit subdued. But, on their way to a 14-8 success, Scotland scored a spectacular try when seven players handled the ball before MacMyn plunged over near the post.

The sun shone for the opening of the Murrayfield Stadium and the 70,000 spectators were to be rewarded with a thrilling encounter. Ireland remembers vividly the noise and the passion with which the match was played.

England scored first with a penalty by Luddington, then a Macpherson break made a try for Nelson which Drysdale converted. Before half-time R. H. Hamilton-Wickes crossed for England and Luddington added the goal points. When English captain, W. W. Wakefield, added another English try, things were not going according to the script. Scotland were given a let-off by the Welsh referee, Mr Freethy, when MacMyn was allowed an early charge on the conversion attempt. Thus relieved, Johnny Wallace sprinted over at the other end and Gillies, à la P. C. Brown, thumped over a touch-line conversion. Only a point in it and the tension was almost unbearable. Waddell tried one dropped goal — and missed. The second made history. 'If he had missed that time we would have killed him,' says Ireland.

There were no civic receptions, no invitations to No 10, no after-the-match Press conferences. Jimmy swopped his jersey and, later, received a bill for the new one, from Aitken and Niven, for 12s. 6d. Ireland became the London manager of Scottish and Newcastle Breweries, an international referee, a member of the SRU committee, a selector, a member of the International Board and the president of the Union in 1950-51. His cap he sent to the museum in Cape Town; his memories live briskly on in Polmont.

There were many false dawns before Scotland could celebrate again. The Jimmy Ireland squad — if such a modern description can be applied to such a side — won three of their four internationals in 1926, failing to repeat their previous year's

CHAMPAGNE IN THE MURRAYFIELD DRESSING-ROOM AFTER THE 1984 GRAND SLAM WIN OVER THE FRENCH... EDINBURGH
LORD PROVOST, TOM MORGAN, IS THE MAN DOING THE HONOURS

PERFECT POISE. PETER DODS ABOUT TO SLOT ANOTHER ONE BETWEEN THE STICKS

triumph by losing only 3-0 at home to Ireland, with an injury-time try when the Scots were down to 14 men. In 1927, with Dan Drysdale, John Bannerman, Herbert Waddell and Ireland still very much in evidence, they did the same again, this time losing 6-0 in a gale-lashed Dublin. Two of the Irish players collapsed and the referee, it was reported, had a 'lifeless left hand'. One hopes he was not a corry-fister.

Six years later Scotland, under the captaincy of Ian Smith in his last season, took revenge, clinching the Triple Crown with an 8-6 victory in Dublin thanks to a Harry Lind dropped goal. Alas, there was to be no chance of a Grand Slam as the Scots and the French rugby authorities had suspended relations, the former not too happy about the 'amateur' spirit of the latter; *plus ca change* . . . ! For the same reason Wilson Shaw's Triple Crowners of 1938 were denied their shot at the full house. By 1984 Shaw, one of the best-loved presidents the SRU ever produced, had gone to his ancestors but his widow was at the vital game in Dublin. The SRU, by the way, patched up their quarrel with the French and sportingly agreed to resume the fixture in Paris in January 1940. Hitler had other ideas.

When the boys came home there were a few other priorities and the championship did not resume in full until 1947. Scotland lost every game that year, had a magnificent, if unexpected success over Wales in 1951, then crashed to 17 successive defeats, including a 44-0 rout by the South Africans at Murrayfield.

The succeeding years often flattered to deceive. Tom Elliot, the Gala prop, will go to his grave convinced he scored the try at Twickenham in 1955 that would have clinched another Triple Crown. The Welsh referee didn't see it that way and England won 9-6. In 1961 Scotland again went to English HQ with a crown in prospect, lost 6-0, and the following year, with Arthur Smith as captain, could only manage a draw with the Auld Enemy when victory was required. The hoodoo struck twice more at Twickenham: in 1973, with the famous Ian McLauchlan broken-leg encounter and, in 1975, with Douglas Morgan missing penalty chances that he would normally have chipped over. So despite the presence of forwards of the calibre of McLauchlan, Sandy Carmichael, Nairn MacEwan and Alastair McHarg, plus world-class backs such as Andy Irvine and Jim Renwick, Scotland arrived in the 1980s without a championship or crown in the cupboard.

Enter James W. Telfer, taking over as coach to the international side from Nairn MacEwan right at the start of the decade. Telfer is Messianic; a man of incredible commitment, ruthless honesty, a figure who inspires fear and love in about equal quantities. Derek White once said: 'I don't know whether I am more afraid to tell my wife that I am going to another squad session or Jim Telfer that I am not.' He didn't miss too many sessions.

Telfer is not a particularly good loser. He wanted to put his club, Melrose, and Scotland on to the top of the pile and, for quite some time, he believed he knew how both these aims could be achieved. The Telfer teams would play in the New

SIMON HALLIDAY COMES TO THE RESCUE OF RICHARD HILL WHO LOOKS AS IF HE'S JUST BEEN BITTEN BY THE WHITE SHARK JOHN JEFFREY. DEREK WHITE IS SET TO MAKE THE NEXT TACKLE

OUCH! DEREK WHITE'S GAME IS ABOUT TO COME TO AN END. SKINNER WILL CRASH INTO THE LONDON SCOTTISH No 8's RIGHT KNEE AND HAWICK'S DEREK TURNBULL WILL BE THE REPLACEMENT

WILL CARLING IS BROUGHT TO HIS KNEES BY JOHN JEFFREY. KEN MILNE, DEREK TURNBULL AND CRAIG CHALMERS ARE THE OTHER SCOTS IN ATTENDANCE

OFFENSIVE DEFENCE. IT IS LATE IN THE SECOND HALF AND THE SCOTS HAVE THEIR BACKS TO THEIR TRY LINE. THE STRAIN TELLS ON THE FACES OF TURNBULL, MILNE AND CALDER. MIKE TEAGUE AND PETER WINTERBOTTOM ARE THE ENGLAND PLAYERS CAUSING THE PROBLEMS

CAPTAIN VICTORIOUS. TARTAN BUNNET ASKEW, A DELIGHTED DAVID SOLE SEEKS THE SAFE HAVEN OF THE POLICE CORDON

A BOTTLE OF BUBBLY FOR SCOTLAND'S TRY HERO TONY STANGER

A MEMENTO OF A MOMENTOUS OCCASION. CRAIG CHALMERS WITH THE AUTOGRAPHED GRAND SLAM MATCH BALL

I WAS THERE! NO NEED TO ASK WHICH TEAM THIS YOUNG CHAP WAS SUPPORTING

THE PRINCESS ROYAL, PRINCESS ANNE, PATRON OF THE SCOTTISH RUGBY UNION, MEETING THE TEAMS PRIOR TO KICK-OFF

CHRIS GRAY THE NOTTINGHAM LOCK IS THE CENTRE OF ATTRACTION

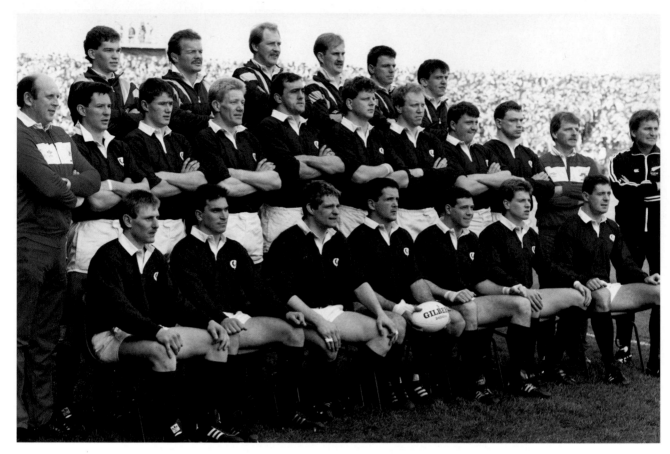

THE SCOTLAND GRAND SLAM LINE-UP, MURRAYFIELD, SATURDAY, 17 MARCH 1990.
BACK ROW (REPLACEMENTS): A. C. REDPATH (MELROSE), A. K. BREWSTER (STEWART'S-MELVILLE FP), D. J. TURNBULL (HAWICK), D. S. WYLLIE (STEWART'S-MELVILLE FP), J. ALLAN (EDINBURGH ACADEMICALS) AND G. H. OLIVER (HAWICK)
MIDDLE ROW: L. J. PEARD (WALES) TOUCH JUDGE, S. R. P. LINEEN (BOROUGHMUIR),
A. G. STANGER (HAWICK), J. JEFFREY (KELSO), C. A. GRAY (NOTTINGHAM), D. F. CRONIN (BATH),
D. B. WHITE (LONDON SCOTTISH), A. P. BURNELL (LONDON SCOTTISH), K. S. MILNE (HERIOT'S FP),
W. D. BEVAN (WALES) TOUCH JUDGE, D. J. BISHOP (NEW ZEALAND) REFEREE
FRONT ROW: G. ARMSTRONG (JED-FOREST), I. TUKALO (SELKIRK), F. CALDER (STEWART'S-MELVILLE FP), D. M. B. SOLE (EDINBURGH ACADEMICALS) CAPTAIN, S. HASTINGS (WATSONIANS), C. M. CHALMERS (MELROSE), A. G. HASTINGS (LONDON SCOTTISH)

ENGLAND FLANKER MICKEY SKINNER GETS DOWN TO IT. GARY ARMSTRONG, CHRIS GRAY AND IWAN TUKALO FANCY A PIECE OF THE ACTION TOO

THE ENGLAND LINE-UP. *BACK ROW*: M. D. BAILEY (WASPS), J. M. WEBB (BATH), S. M. BATES (WASPS),
D. W. EGERTON (BATH), M. S. LINNETT (MOSELEY), C. J. OLVER (HARLEQUINS)
MIDDLE ROW: BEN GILLFEATHER (ENGLAND) TEAM DOCTOR, S. J. HALLIDAY (BATH), W. A. DOOLEY (PRESTON
GRASSHOPPERS), M. G. SKINNER (HARLEQUINS), P. J. ACKFORD (HARLEQUINS), J. A. PROBYN (WASPS),
P. A. G. RENDALL (WASPS), M. G. TEAGUE (GLOUCESTER), P. J. WINTERBOTTOM (HARLEQUINS),
W. D. BEVAN (WALES) TOUCH JUDGE, D. J. BISHOP (NEW ZEALAND) REFEREE
FRONT ROW: R. J. HILL (BATH), S. D. HODGKINSON (NOTTINGHAM), R. UNDERWOOD (LEICESTER AND RAF), W. D. C. CARLING
(HARLEQUINS) CAPTAIN, B. C. MOORE (NOTTINGHAM), J. C. GUSCOTT (BATH), C. R. ANDREW (WASPS)

IT'S IN THERE SOMEWHERE. SCOTLAND PROP PAUL BURNELL TAKES A 'WEE KEEK' OVER THE TOP AS CHRIS GRAY ADOPTS A
LOFTIER POSE. A NEEDLE AND THREAD WOULD APPEAR TO BE REQUIRED FOR ONE OF THE ENGLAND FORWARDS

SCOTLAND'S SEAN LINEEN HAS THE MISFORTUNE TO FALL INTO THE CLUTCHES OF ENGLAND NO 8 MIKE TEAGUE. SKINNER, WINTERBOTTOM, CARLING AND ANDREW ARE IN CLOSE ATTENDANCE WHILE THE SCOTTISH CAVALRY ARRIVES IN THE FORM OF CALDER AND ARMSTRONG

GARY ARMSTRONG, WHO HAS NEVER PLAYED A BETTER GAME FOR SCOTLAND, ABOUT TO DEPART THE SCENE DESPITE THE INTENTIONS OF OPPOSITE NUMBER RICHARD HILL

Zealand style. In the late 1960s I heard Telfer speaking at a Royal High FP dinner about the need for Scotland to adopt a rucking style. He might have been talking in Chinese; but as he began to put his theory into practice his disciples grew. Quite simply he wanted the ball put on the ground at the point of breakdown and for the forwards to drive over it, allowing quick release. That's it.

Telfer took the Scots to New Zealand in 1981 and, although both Tests were lost, the first at Dunedin was only by 11-4. The coach himself believes to this day that one of Scotland's finest post-war performances was a win over Canterbury on that tour. The bond was beginning to form. The next season Scotland played six internationals, won four, drew one and lost to Ireland. In 1982 they won their first Test in the Southern Hemisphere beating Australia 12-7 in Brisbane.

But Telfer was then destined for an even stiffer examination; he was named as coach to the British Lions tour of New Zealand in 1983. Eight Scots went with him but as the All Blacks won all four Tests, the last by 38-6, it could hardly be called a successful safari. Jim admits he returned home bitterly disappointed but recalls: 'On the plane back John Rutherford told me he thought Scotland could win the Triple Crown the next season.' For his view the fly-half's sanity was questioned. Yet Telfer was far from broken and immediately resumed as the Scottish coach.

By now, however, and almost by accident, he had a captain with whom he was entirely in tune. Andy Irvine had been Scotland's skipper when Telfer first took over; they liked and respected each other. But Irvine was two things which Telfer could not come to terms with — he was unpredictable and he was a back. Jim Aitken was neither. Known to the players as 'Big Daddy', Jim Aitken was unlikely to be the ideal partner for the débutantes' ball. The Gala prop was a mean machine. Telfer knew immediately he could work with him. 'He carried out my instructions to the letter. He understood what I wanted him to do. And he made sure the players did as well. Aitken was already a successful club captain and a national leader.'

Ironically Telfer's troops were to face the visiting All Blacks at Murrayfield in November 1983. A thrilling 25-25 draw entertained the crowd but the coach was far from satisfied. 'We were a bit lucky and it wasn't their full side. Still we fought well.'

The first championship game was in the once-dreaded National Stadium in Cardiff. But Scotland had laid that bogey back in 1982 with Roger Baird lighting the fuse with his famous run out of defence. This was an uneasy, sometimes dirty, encounter in which the Scots hung on well to win by 15-9. 'It wasn't unlike the match in Cardiff this year,' says Telfer, 'we defended well and kept our discipline. The deciding try came from Big Daddy himself, Roy Laidlaw feeding Aitken who barged over with a little added momentum from David Leslie who booted his skipper on the backside.' Most importantly, as he would all season, Peter Dods, at last free from Irvine's shadow, would kick his goals. Telfer persuaded his fellow selectors that the team should be retained *en bloc* for the next game at Murrayfield, the 100th international between England and Scotland.

This was John Rutherford's match, a brilliant display of tactical kicking destroying the England full-back Dusty Hare. 'We knew all about Hare's weaknesses,' said Telfer laconically, 'he was on the Lions tour.' Poor Dusty was not only drawn like a puppet on a string from one side of the field to the other but his goal-kicking skills deserted him. He missed four penalties in the first half before putting one over just before half-time. After the interval he managed only one out of three.

Meanwhile Scotland had gone ahead with a David Johnston try, nudging the ball past Hare and dribbling over to score. The former professional soccer player swears to this day that he never said 'I controlled it with my left and put it away with my right', but if he didn't, he should have. The other try-scorer was also a Watsonian. Euan Kennedy took a Rutherford pass and crashed through for the touch-down of his life. Sadly he soon had to go off with knee ligament trouble but the Myreside celebrations went on long into the night.

All that remained was for Peter Dods to kick his goals and Scotland were home 18-6. The chairman of the Scottish selectors, Ian MacGregor, complained that his side had given away too many penalties: 'There was too much minor indiscipline and talking back to the referee.' Still, they were, although resolutely not thinking about it, halfway to the Grand Slam.

So let's pause again and look, through Telfer's eye, at the 1984 squad.

'Iain Milne was a key forward. The Bear was at the height of his powers and though he took quite a hammering at times he never conceded anything. Nor did he resort to retaliation.

'David Leslie was another — he had an outstanding season and his ability to get the ball at the back of the line was a terrific asset. The back row of Jim Calder, Iain Paxton and Leslie worked in unity with the world-class half-backs, Rutherford and Laidlaw.

'No one should forget either the contributions of Alan Tomes and Bill Cuthbertson and latterly ''Sally'' Campbell of Hawick. Colin Deans was much more than just a hooker, his speed about the field and his throwing in were vital.

'I suppose some people would say it was not Scotland's greatest-ever three-quarters line but both Watsonians and Keith Robertson did the job they were there to do. Roger Baird, Steve Munro and Jim Pollock all had their moment while Dods was the man who gave us the victories with his utterly reliable ball-kicking.'

The Irish were convinced Scotland were going to clinch the Triple Crown in Dublin. When we arrived at the airport, ties and scarves bearing that legend were already on sale. Ireland's captain, Willie Duggan, seemed to concur when he won the toss and astonishingly gave Scotland the wind.

By half-time the Scots were 22-0 ahead and the contest was over. This was Roy Laidlaw's match, although he played in only half of it. Twice, the Jed Forest terrier tore open the Irish defence for tries before he had to retire with a head knock. Dods kicked a couple of penalties then referee Fred Howard awarded Scotland a penalty try after Willie Duggan had dived into the visiting scrum. Gordon Hunter of Selkirk came on for Laidlaw, winning his first full cap.

GARY ARMSTRONG FOLLOWS THE FLIGHT OF THE BALL IN THIS SHOT FROM THE IRELAND MATCH AT LANSDOWNE ROAD

GREIG OLIVER SERVES HIS STAND-OFF IN THIS HAWICK V KELSO ENCOUNTER FROM 1987

For a while in the second half Ireland rallied with a penalty and a Michael Kiernan try. But Keith Robertson claimed another try and Dods rounded it off with a magnificent score into injury time. The Scots had won handsomely 32-9 and there was a warm round of applause when Telfer, Aitken and MacGregor appeared in the Press room. 'We had a month's break since the England game and the pressure had started to build on the players,' said the coach. 'In these circumstances to score five tries away from home was a tremendous performance.'

Only now did the Grand Slam implications begin to be felt and already there were worries. Laidlaw was under observation in a Dublin hospital and the unlucky Hunter had collided with a small boy running off the field, the Selkirk scrum-half ending up with a depressed fracture of his cheek. Hunter would certainly not play against France on 17 March and doubts were freely expressed about Laidlaw's chances. The selectors began to scour around; Douglas Morgan, last capped six years earlier but still doing the business for Stewart's-Melville, was asked if he would make himself available. Morgan agreed but Laidlaw was not to be denied the moment of glory.

The French came to Murrayfield also intent on clinching the Slam. They were a side capable of dazzling inventiveness . . . and ill-discipline. Almost immediately in the clinching match they developed a hate-hate relationship with Welsh referee, Winston Jones. As the Welshman's arm went up time and again, Dods, despite a black and rapidly closing eye, slammed over the penalties — five in all. The final moment, encapsulated forever in Ronnie Browne's fine painting, is of Jim Calder plunging over for the decisive try from a lineout. There is incredulity and surliness on every French face — joy on every Scots. In France they were to dub the match 'The Grand Steal' — in Scotland they were too intent on celebrating to care.

The players were swept off into a dizzy round of social engagements, taken to Edinburgh Castle, to the City Chambers, to dinners large and small. Ties, scarves, jumpers, hats, books, banners and special television programmes were produced. 'The Grand Slam,' David Leslie was heard to mutter, 'has become the Great Rip-off.' Certainly there had been more emotion in Ireland than there was after the French success. The players' 'reward' was a dreadful tour later that year to pre-revolutionary Romania where 'Lucky' Jim Pollock experienced defeat for the first time in his international career. The triumphant captain, Jim Aitken, was unceremoniously discarded the following season when Scotland failed to win a single championship game, and Telfer also went into temporary hibernation, concentrating on his career as a head teacher and hotelier.

But for all that, 1984 had been a thrilling experience for any Scot and just to have been at all four games was a matter of pride. Bill Cuthbertson, who missed the last two matches because of injury, summed up the feeling when he said: 'It was wonderful — I just went into the dressing-room and had a good greet.'

How would the 1984 squad compare with the Grand Slam side of six years later? Telfer will not make that comparison. What he does say is: 'I think it was harder for the first team because it had been so long since it had been done. And because they had me as a coach!' The rest of us need not have any such inhibitions and it is always fun to speculate. If you had all the players from both squads available for selection what would be your first choice? This is where you make a few friends and a lot of enemies.

Gavin Hastings would be my full-back though we would have to hope this was one of his good kicking days. Tony Stanger is raw and I would love the experience of Keith Robertson but the big Hawick lad has an awful lot of tries to come. Roger Baird, who never got one for Scotland, would be my left-wing — his chasing and defence were always underrated. I'd pick two Watsonians, the quicksilver David Johnston and the explosive Scott Hastings as the centres. No contest for the half-backs, Craig Chalmers and Gary Armstrong are a superb pairing but they should be glad they did not live in the playing era of Rutherford and Laidlaw. David Sole has to be the captain, he is the best prop Scotland has produced since Ian McLauchlan. Colin Deans would hook and 'The Bear' would be on the other side which, if he has his way, will happen in the next World Cup. He is delighted to have made the tour party to New Zealand this year. The locks are tricky and Chris Gray has improved enormously this season but I'm going for Alan Tomes, who always knew how to look after himself and Damian Cronin because he gets about the park so well. Frankly, picking a back row from the available talent is a nightmare. How could anyone possibly leave out John Jeffrey after the England game? Well I have, going for Finlay Calder, Iain Paxton — we must have some ball at the lineout — and David Leslie.

This is my side: G. Hastings, A. Stanger, D. Johnston, S. Hastings, R. Baird, J. Rutherford, R. Laidlaw, D. Sole (captain), C. Deans, I. Milne, A. Tomes, D. Cronin, F. Calder, I. Paxton, D. Leslie. We are prepared to take on all-comers.

WHERE NOW?

The game has changed enormously since Jimmy Ireland and his mates met for lunch on the day of the match. They travelled second class on the train, had no numbers on their jerseys and if they were even seen talking to a rugby league scout they would risk the wrath of the SRU.

By Aitken's Slam in 1984 the build-up was much more, dare we say, professional. Squads gathered on the Thursdays before internationals and were put up in plush hotels or country clubs; sometimes the forwards were pulled in on a Wednesday. Sunday sessions were commonplace. Now the team received all the kit, from track suits to boots, from one commercial sponsor or another. Players were in great demand to open stores, sign books, speak at dinners. But there was still no sign of any payment.

The 1987 World Cup and the Lions tour of Australia last year opened up a lot of Scottish players' eyes. They discovered that All Blacks were forever popping up on television, advertising goods, or even themselves; Australian players admitted they had had their mortgages paid and had gone to Italy for huge sums. France have always had a unique brand of 'amateurism' — if their players were not exactly paid they were well looked after, often set up in business by grateful supporters. In Wales, boot-money scandals were rife and players were receiving cash from carpark receipts; the English moved clubs for no explicable reason other than some form of incentive.

Meanwhile money was being tipped into the game from every angle. All internationals are sponsored, as are the leagues, and the district championship. Rival TV companies are battling for rights and the demand and the availability of tickets for the major events is a tout's dream. Several Scottish players received invitations to go to the South African Centenary celebrations last year. Only Keith Robertson went — plus a bus-load of officials — but the Scottish Lions knew they could command substantial benefits in cash or kind. They decided they didn't want that kind of reward. Robertson, it should be said, received no money to my knowledge and, sadly, was injured in his first game.

Finlay Calder became the spokesman for the Scottish players. He went to an SRU committee meeting and told the officials they were not living in the real world. 'Only Ireland and ourselves are playing to the amateur rules, the rest are cheating.' Calder made it clear, then and subsequently, that the players did not want paid for playing. 'Rugby has the potential for players to seriously injure one another and a win bonus could be too much of a temptation.' What he and his team-mates wanted the right to do was to sell themselves — write books, open supermarkets, speak at functions. More importantly they wished compensation, for themselves or for their employers, for time spent on rugby duties . . . not just overseas tours but every squad session.

The SRU listened because they knew the matter was coming up at the International Board. A two-man committee was formed, with Sir Ewart Bell of Ireland and Gordon Masson of Scotland told to report. Their recommendations were broadly in line with Calder's argument although there was to be no individual advertising.

At a Board meeting just a fortnight after the 1990 Grand Slam match, a compromise was hammered out. Players who lose money from their jobs by turning out for their country will be able to claim up to £80 per match in compensation. The new rules apply to all 21 members of the squad and four officials. On the question of payment for 'extra mural' activities, the Board is prolonging its investigation. A working party hopes to report in October.

It is interesting to compare the differing attitudes of Jimmy Ireland, Jim Telfer and Finlay Calder on this subject. 'I wouldn't pay them anything,' said Ireland, 'this is meant to be a game played for enjoyment by many, not for reward by some. Maybe internationals have had too much emphasis placed upon them.

'We used to have a joke in our day — if your golf interferes with your business, give up your business. If rugby is taking up too much of the top players' time, maybe they should find a less demanding sport.' He laughed: 'Yes I know I am an old die-hard but that is my honest opinion. Mind you, no one listens to old boys like me and that is probably just as well.'

Jim Telfer takes the middle road: 'You see I believe rugby is a community asset,

DAVID SOLE, NOW RECOGNISED AS A GENUINELY WORLD-CLASS LOOSE-HEAD PROP-FORWARD, SETS THE PATTERN FOR
THE 1990s WITH HIS DYNAMIC DISPLAYS IN OPEN PLAY

particularly in rural areas in that it binds diffuse people in a common aim. The spirit of the club or the town is interchangeable and it works, for the general good, in the cities as well. There is also a great social side to rugby. They say I am not a very sociable type but I enjoy the crack as much as any. Now you professionalise this and a few people at the top will make money. Mind you, there are not too many superstores to be opened in the Borders. But will the club secretary, the selectors, the bloke who runs the touch, the tea ladies, will they then want to be paid too?

'I would not accept, as a coach, if a player said to me he couldn't come to an extra session because he was taking money for speaking at a dinner. So, I go along with the Board's new position. Players should not lose money for appearing for their country. But that, at the moment, is as far as I am prepared to go.'

Finlay Calder still believes there will be more pressure for change. 'I don't think the All Blacks and the Australians or the French will stick to these laws any more than they did to the last lot. No one that I know wants to be paid for playing. But when the stars of the show receive less than the cleaners, that cannot be right. If someone wants to pay John Jeffrey or Scott Hastings to open a video shop I can't see how that hurts rugby.'

Myself, I believe that there will be further relaxations of the amateur code in the future. After all, Scotland, Ireland and England are the only voting members of the International Board actually opposed to implementing in full the Bell-Masson suggestions.

I respect Jim Telfer's sincerity but disagree with his conclusions. Golf clubs did not become less sociable places because people were paid for playing the game, cricket has not disappeared from village greens because the England team is professional, Wimbledon did not become just another tournament when the All-England club finally agreed to have prize money. It is unrealistic, and extremely unjust to expect rugby players to be the only amateur athletes in international sport. Nor is that the case today. I think we have to accept that rugby, played at international level, is different, that the commitment has to be greater and that the demands will grow on the participants as the game increases in popularity. In a decade's time I expect to see a form of payment, probably a trust fund, being introduced.

International squads may well decide, as the New Zealanders did on their last tour, to pool all the 'takings' from a season and share them out. They will probably have agents attached to the squad with the specific role of exploiting marketing opportunities.

England already have a team manager; by the year 2000 I expect the man in this job to be picking the side single-handed as Jacques Fouroux has already been doing in France. Ian McGeechan or Jim Telfer have to produce the goods, why should they have to settle for someone else's team? That is not to say that Bob Munro or any other chairman of selectors has done a bad job. But the manager/coach of the future will also be paid and his job will be on the line. There will be structural changes in the unions themselves — to ensure that they operate more

efficiently. Part-time administrators cannot be expected to give up more and more of their time to run a growing business. Who would want to be a ticket convener?

Now all of this speculation will horrify the purists who will argue that such changes will destroy the game of rugby as we know it. They said exactly the same thing about the numbered jerseys, no kicking to touch outside the 25 law and the introduction of the league system. Nothing stands still forever. I agree with Jim Telfer when he says rugby is a character-building sport; it will remain so whether or not a few, because that is what we are talking about, of its brightest stars are being paid what they are worth.

But here's a strange thing . . . I agree with Jimmy Ireland as well — we never should have changed that playing the ball with your foot after a tackle law!

To both, my sincere thanks for co-operating in this chapter. To both, the nation's gratitude for providing us with the stuff of dreams.

Chapter Six

MEETING THEIR MAKERS

By DEREK DOUGLAS

MEETING THEIR MAKERS

THE HEADLINE IN AN ENGLISH NEWSPAPER was indeed inspired. 'England To Meet Their Maker', it read. But it didn't denote that the English rugby squad had been pencilled in for an early appointment with the Almighty. It referred to the fact that the core of the England team which was to perform on Grand Slam Saturday at Murrayfield — Rob Andrew, Jeremy Guscott, Rory Underwood, and in particular the locks, Wade Dooley and Paul Ackford, hooker, Brian Moore and No 8 Mike Teague — had blossomed under coach Ian McGeechan's tutelage during the victorious British Lions' tour to Australia the previous summer. McGeechan, Lions skipper, Finlay Calder and the England coach, Roger Uttley, had fashioned a team of steely resolve in the Antipodes to make a superb comeback and secure the series by two Tests to one. In so doing the Leeds schoolmaster (Geography and PE at Fir Tree Middle School) who played 32 games at stand-off and centre for Scotland and who took part in two Lions' tours, to South Africa and New Zealand, confirmed his position as the world's top rugby coach.

He was appointed coach to the Scotland side in 1988 having been assistant coach to Derrick Grant of Hawick for three years during which time he also coached Scotland B. The continuity and calibre of the Scottish coaching staff is underlined when one considers that McGeechan was assisted in his duties this season by Grant, Jim Telfer, who coached the 1984 Scotland Grand Slam side (and who, just a week before the Slam match, had coached Melrose to their first National Leagues Division One title), and Douglas Morgan of Stewart's-Melville, the former Scotland and British Lions' scrum-half.

McGeechan is a quietly spoken Yorkshire Scot (with the dialect to match) who thinks deeply about the game of rugby football. He confirmed shortly after the Grand Slam win that he would coach the Scotland side during the summer tour to New Zealand when the European champions would be pitted against the world champion All Blacks. This, though, would take him away from his wife, Judy, son, Robert (11) and daughter, Heather (six) for a second summer. Consider also the number of nights spent away at squad sessions, selection meetings and so on and the dedication of the man, and the understanding of his wife, can be appreciated.

'I suppose you could say that we don't have much of a social life. No, correct that. We don't have any social life at all. Luckily, my wife is a full-time student just now so she gets some student life during the day. But yes, it is very time consuming and virtually all-enveloping.'

McGeechan is a quiet, self-contained man, seemingly at one with the world and an oasis of calm when under pressure. Scotland's 1990 Grand Slam was — and he would be the very last to admit it — as much a triumph for him and the Scotland coaching team as it was for the young men who carried the colours on the pitch. Scotland's performance in the Calcutta Cup match was just about as clinical a display as will ever be seen. That clear-cut style and ruthless efficiency is a credit to the work which was put in on the back pitches at Murrayfield during many a windy winter Sunday and weekday night.

Here, in an extended interview conducted just four days after the greatest day in Scottish rugby history, Ian McGeechan talks in depth about the preparation that went into the Grand Slam match, about the unique bond between himself and his fellow Scotland coaches, and about his general coaching philosophy.

When did you start laying plans in earnest for the Calcutta Cup game?

The Monday immediately after the Welsh match. Following that game we wanted to look at our own performance and determine what things we needed to change. Jim, Derrick, Dougie and myself all took things to look at. Derrick was looking at lineouts, as he had done against the Irish at Lansdowne Road, and Jim was looking at the forward play and possession. Dougie was particularly interested in the half-backs while I was looking at the use of possession.

Was there anything giving you specific cause for concern?

We knew we had to try and use our possession to build an attacking platform and to try and keep the game more continuous than the game in Cardiff had been. But we also realised that playing Wales in their particular frame of mind at that time, with the resignation of their coach, the appointment of Ron Waldron and the injection of Neath players and so on, was always going to be difficult. They were on a very high emotional plateau at that time. We knew it would be a stern test and it was.

What were Scotland's specific strengths?

We were quite pleased with our ball-winning ability and the control that we were starting to get into the games. And obviously our defensive qualities had started to improve since last year. I think that we are very much a full team defensively.

If you haven't got the ball then the most important thing is to get it back again

110

JIM TELFER...NOW ASSISTANT COACH TO IAN McGEECHAN BUT A GRAND SLAM-WINNING COACH IN HIS OWN RIGHT

ROGER UTTLEY...GOOD LUCK TO SCOTLAND, BUT THIS
DEFEAT HAS CAUSED US MUCH GRIEF

DERRICK GRANT...THE EX-HAWICK, SCOTLAND AND BRITISH LIONS
FLANKER WHO HAS BEEN AN INVALUABLE MEMBER OF
THE SCOTTISH COACHING STAFF

and if you merely accept that other teams, when they have won it, are going to have the space and time to do the things they want then you will always be in trouble. One of the ways we always try to approach defensive play is to say, well we don't happen to have the ball just now but it is our intention to get it back as quickly as possible.

Were there any weaknesses in England's game that you particularly wanted to concentrate on?

No, not particularly. England had played very well and they had given good all-round performances, particularly in France where their play that day was outstanding. It was not so much looking for weaknesses against England, more of looking at patterns which they used and targeting key players.

We always knew the set pieces were going to be crucial. England had put pressure on every other team at scrum and lineout. That was where we had to be as secure as we had ever been. Plus, we had to try to break down the routines that England hoped to use at the lineout. We planned to move our jumpers around, change our own formats. Our strategy didn't have to match the patterns that had been available before. Derrick and Jim spent a lot of time looking at the lineout after the Ireland game where we hadn't done very well. We all felt that, come the Calcutta Cup match, we had to be on top of our game, thinking quickly and giving ourselves a greater number of options where we could get quick access to the ball. You have to try and grasp the initiative in every way possible. By moving our lineout jumpers around that was one way of doing it psychologically where you could just get a little edge. If you can get that crucial edge just two or three times then it just puts a different picture and perspective on the game.

That marvellous slow march on to the pitch. How did that come about?

That was the players' idea. They actually wanted a piper as well! The thinking behind it was that it would have been easy, in view of what both teams had done before, for some people to think that the game meant more to England than to us. The point was that it was the Grand Slam and it was important for both sides. The players wanted to make that point. We were playing at home and they wanted to make sure that everybody in the ground realised that they were going out to win a Grand Slam. They wanted to show everybody that that was what they were there for. It certainly got a reaction from the crowd immediately and it continued longer than it would have done if they had just run out in the normal fashion.

And what about the singing of 'Flower of Scotland'?

Well it was just incredible. We've all heard the singing at Cardiff but for sheer emotion and intensity of feeling that was unique. I've never heard anything like it before.

Do you think the England players ever really recovered from the emotional battering they received before the game had even started?

Well, I wouldn't go as far as that but it certainly made it perfectly plain to them that they weren't playing at home and, however many English were there, there were definitely 50,000 Scots at Murrayfield and that was made particularly obvious to the English in the early stages. The fact that we were so positive in the first four or five phases of the game just generated an even greater reaction from the crowd that had started with 'Flower of Scotland'.

I have never experienced anything like the involvement of a crowd like that one. Just sat in the stand there, I remember when Gavin kicked to touch late in the second half and the team made its way along the touch-line to the lineout, each section of the crowd was standing and applauding as the team moved upfield. The players must have got a lift from that — well I know they did. Afterwards they said they just saw all those faces and heard the cheers and the clapping. It was a wonderful experience for them.

You knew Roger Uttley, the England coach, from last summer in Australia. Similarly you knew the strengths and weaknesses of a lot of the England players from that tour. Did that help or hinder you in your preparations?

I did not really consider too greatly what had happened in Australia because the circumstances out there were so different. What it did do for myself and the Scottish Lions was to instil an immediate respect for the English players because they had been so good in Australia under pressure. The tendency sometimes is that because it's the Auld Enemy we can just go out and beat them. But there was, this time, a greater awareness amongst the players about the ability that England had shown, and a greater respect for their players. In the end that was probably as great an influencing factor as anything we had talked about or done in Australia. We were all very aware of how well they had played and of course it had been shown in the games leading up to ours.

After the match, the former Welsh international, Eddie Butler, said on TV that if it had been Ian McGeechan's intention to plan chaos then he had succeeded supremely well. Did you take that as a compliment?

No I didn't, because it suggests that everything we did was totally negative and that was very far from the truth. If you take the first ten or 15 minutes of the game we were totally positive with every ball we won. England got no look-in at all. They had to tackle us, we were scrummaging them, they had to beat us at the lineout. There was nothing negative there. We were going for points. We were going for tries.

For me, one of the highlights was the fearsome drive from Finlay Calder which led to the first successful Scottish penalty goal.

Yes, that was magnificent. Play like that was beginning to set the pattern and these little psychological things maybe get the opposition thinking a certain way. I think it was the clarity with which the Scottish players were seeing the game at that stage that was encouraging. I was encouraged also by the way that the ball was being used and the way our players were supporting one another and in the way they were taking the game to England.

Earlier you mentioned it had been part of your build-up to target key opposition players. Who did you consider England's key players were?

Well, I don't want to go into individual cases. But, as I've said, the lineout was crucial to us and the scrums. We had to be particularly competitive in these two phases of play. Also, if we had lost the ball, then the first tackles were crucial. So obviously around the fringes and in the centre field, the defence had to be absolutely right on the day. Not just in ones but in twos and threes.

If we had had an intent to stop Wales playing, and we did, then it had to be double that intent against England because, you know, we saw in the try they scored just how quickly they could move a ball and raise the pace of the game once they had a little bit of room.

Were you ever able to relax at any point during the game?

Never. I never relaxed at all and the more the game went on the greatest worry was that it was going to end up a 13-13 draw. And that would have been such an anti-climax. I did, though, feel comfortable by the way that England were playing in the last 15 minutes because I felt then that we were dictating how the game should be played and I thought, well, it augurs well for us that we are not allowing them to get into the lines and patterns that they had been able to do in previous games.

And then there was that amazing episode late on when England were really threatening. Skinner and the England back row were on the drive and then Will Carling was held up inside the Scotland 22 and driven back ten metres.

That just epitomised the whole performance. There we were, we had lost the ball and yet we ended up going 30 yards out of defence.

In more general terms, how do you motivate players to deliver more than perhaps even they think they can achieve at that kind of world level?

Well, I can assure you motivation wasn't a problem against England. The greatest worry was that players were going to be so uptight that they wouldn't actually think about the game they would have to play to beat England. On the field, tactically, they had to get it right if they were going to beat England. If we had done things which allowed England into the game then they were a good enough side to snap up every opportunity. So the greatest worry was, tactically, keeping the game the way we wanted it played.

114

DOUGLAS MORGAN...THE WILY EX-INTERNATIONAL SCRUM-HALF HAD PARTICULAR COACHING RESPONSIBILITY FOR THE HALF-BACKS

BOB MUNRO...CHAIRMAN OF THE SELECTORS THROUGHOUT THE GRAND SLAM CAMPAIGN, WITH A PREVIOUS SCOTLAND SKIPPER, COLIN DEANS. THE SUBJECT UNDER DISCUSSION APPEARS TO BE HAWICK BALLS!

Which was?

Really just along the lines we have been discussing, working to make sure of certain areas, like scrum and lineout, and ensuring that, with the ball or without it, we would try to take the game to England.

How do you instil mental hardness into a player? It will be relatively easy to hone a player to perfection physically but at the level you are operating on, people have got to be mentally fit as well.

It is possible to train for that to a certain extent. We have upped the intensity of our training sessions now. They are much faster, more aggressive and require greater concentration, even in the warm-up practices. A lot of the grid work and speed work is with a ball in close-quarter situations where the players have to concentrate every time they catch or pass a ball. You have to get it right because if you do something wrong then you put five or six other players wrong. Now that is, I think, where we have come on.

For instance, at a squad session you might be simply talking to players or having a fairly light warm-up and then you are into one of these intensive sessions and they have got to be able to switch on and not make mistakes. That has been important in pointing out to the players the very high level of concentration they have to produce.

Yourself and Jim Telfer are very different types of characters. You seem to be quite relaxed and laid back whereas Jim is a very intense individual. Do you think your different personalities complement each other?

Well, I think Jim has done more for Scottish rugby than anyone else I can think of. We are where we are now because of what he started in 1980. I have had the good fortune to work with Derrick Grant and then with Jim, and I have learned a lot from both of them. I just can't give them enough credit for where we are now.

People say, well they're Borderers and what could you have in common with them? I don't really know, but I do know that, as men, I genuinely like them. We get on and talk easily. I think the important thing is that we all talk on the same lines. We all believe in the same things. So, even when we are separate in the training sessions, we are not going in diverse directions. Jim and Derrick are very intense and very aggressive in their approach to the forwards because the forwards have to perform that way. The worst thing for me would be to try to be a Jim Telfer or a Derrick Grant because I just couldn't do it. I couldn't match what they do. Jim said what we have now, with Dougie Morgan as well, is a perspective on the game from four viewpoints which means that generally we end up with a very good overview of what we should be doing. Therefore it is quite easy for me to draw everything together because we are all on the same wavelength.

Sometimes at dinner after an international we won't leave the dining table, we'll just sit and talk rugby for three or four hours and all the time it's an education for all of us in clarifying what we want to do and where we think we are going. I think in some respects the relationship we have is quite unique.

Do Morgan and Grant have any official standing just now?

Well, I suppose they are just called assistant coaches. Jim and I run the two sessions although Derrick is involved with the lineout and Dougie particularly looks at the half-backs. When the backs are working then Dougie and I will be stood together just comparing what we have seen and deciding whether or not something should be different. All the time you have someone to bounce ideas off. Jim and Derrick are the same.

When we come together, the team session is run by Jim and myself or Jim will look at the forwards and I will be looking at the pattern of what we want to play and I have to decide where the priorities are for the next game and things like that.

Does it annoy you when critics, mainly south of the Border, say that Scotland is just a kick and rush side? They say it disparagingly.

We try and do well what we think we are good at. I would defy anybody to say that we kicked and rushed against Ireland and Wales last year in particular. We have a plan that we would like to see the side play to. The important thing this year was that we had to come into the championship last so all the other sides had a game under their belt. We were meeting every side on the rebound from having a thrashing by England and so there was more of a mental and psychological pressure on us this year. We were one of the favourites and here we were coming in last and having to prove it against very difficult opposition, especially Wales and Ireland who were back in front of their own crowds and trying to prove to them that the games against England had been a one-off and they were better than that.

If it had been Ireland or Wales who had been playing as well as England have been this season and it had been either of them that Scotland were meeting at Murrayfield for the Grand Slam do you think there would have been the same outcome? By that I mean, at least so far as the crowd was concerned, it was important that it was the Auld Enemy we had to beat.

I know what you mean. A very obvious influence on the game, and how it was perceived by Scotland supporters, was the size of the English Press. The game was going to get a greater priority, hype, than it would if we were playing Ireland or France for the Grand Slam. There was greater intensity even than for the 1984 Grand Slam because of the way that the game had been presented in the media in the previous two weeks. In that respect we were very aware of the game and situation. Obviously the greatest number of Press and followers and everything else belongs to England.

We knew we were into the most difficult game of the season so you could see why people and the Press reacted in the way they did. The rugby England had been playing, though, was genuinely outstanding.

Did the England camp begin to believe their own publicity?

No, I don't think they did. There is a level-headedness about them now. Knowing Will Carling and Brian Moore and Rob Andrew, as I do now, there was a greater level-headedness about them this time around. Certainly, I think, they believed their Press before we played them last year at Twickenham but I think this time they had a much better approach and they knew what was at stake and the manner in which the game was likely to be played.

You will be off this summer to New Zealand with the Scotland touring party. How much pressure does the Scotland job put on your family?

We have no social life. If I am in Scotland every weekend and at weekdays as well we don't see anybody else. Judy, my wife, has no social life at all. The only thing is that she is a full-time student at the moment doing a degree so she does have some student life during the day. But as far as seeing friends or going out is concerned we don't, it's as simple as that. Even on nights I am at home I tend to spend looking at videos of previous matches, jot down notes and so on. I've got school work to do as well so it's all quite hectic. We've also got a young family, Robert, who is 11, and Heather, who is six.

You were just putting Heather to bed before we began this interview.

Yes, you see this is one of the things that's not always appreciated. During the international season I'm away such a lot. I couldn't put her to bed on Sunday night when we got home from Edinburgh because the phone just never stopped ringing. On Monday night I was away when she went to bed. I was away again the following night and that kind of thing gets to her at six years old. I had promised that tonight I would put her to bed, see her down, read her a quick story.

You said you were away on Monday night. You were actually on the BBC's _Wogan_ show. How did that go?

It was fine. He was actually at the game. The interesting thing was that he used hardly any of the questions his researchers had mapped out for him. The producer said he had done the ideal research because he had actually been there. So it just came out spontaneously.

Will Carling, who was on with you, and John Jeffrey seemed to handle defeat quite well. He seemed to take it on the chin.

Yes. I think that is where Will, from last year, has learned a lot. There is no doubt that the England camp was very disappointed on Saturday but for him to come on to TV like that does him a lot of credit.

Finally, if I can return to the Grand Slam game, you were quite canny about what was said to the media about your chances. It now seems that it rather suited the Scots to be underdogs and play that up.

Yes, I was quite happy to be in the position we were in because obviously it was

118

the first game of the season where we were the underdogs so we had nothing really to live up to. Here we were with one game to play and we had won three. England, no matter how they had played before, were in exactly the same position. It was all going to be on the 80 minutes at Murrayfield and, you know, that was the bottom line. It was going to whichever side wanted it most and got it right on the day.

And Scotland did.

Thankfully, the players did.

THE ENGLAND COACH ROGER UTTLEY has, just like his Scotland counterpart, experienced the trials and tribulations of international rugby as a player. A fine forward, whose career succumbed ultimately to a troublesome back injury, Uttley is now a games master at Harrow School.

Six days after that Grand Slam defeat at Murrayfield, Uttley made no attempt to hide his disappointment. However, he promised that England would be back, challenging for honours, next season and that the Murrayfield defeat had been, more or less, just a hiccup in England's preparations for the 1991 World Cup.

I'll start by asking you the same question I asked Ian McGeechan. Were there any special preparations that you undertook for the Calcutta Cup match in particular?

Well, we obviously looked at Scotland's game plan very closely and looked at the areas where we might have to counteract them. We did so bearing in mind our performance at Twickenham against them last year (12-12 draw). As it happened, they performed in a similar fashion at Murrayfield.

Are you referring here to what your manager, Geoff Cooke, has referred to as the 'scavenging' aspect of Scotland play?

Well, certainly they made every attempt to make sure that we couldn't play the game.

And at Murrayfield did they play generally or specifically very much as you expected them to play?

Without a doubt, yes. They showed their tenacity in the tackle situation; their back row pressurised exceptionally well; they infiltrated phases of play really well from the lineout where they stepped through; and they infiltrated in the broken play where they managed to insert bodies beyond the ball.

You seem to be suggesting that Scotland were off-side for most of the time.

I didn't say that. The one thing I don't want to come across is that I begrudge Scotland their victory last Saturday. I mean they played very well but you asked me if we prepared to play Scotland and the answer is yes, we did prepare to play them and what we saw didn't in any way surprise us. The only frustration was that for various reasons we weren't able to come to grips with that style of play.

119

If, as you say, you had prepared specifically to counteract this form of play and that you knew exactly what to expect why, on the day, were the 15 English players not able to put into practice all that you had done and discussed beforehand?

Well, we had the opportunities to do so. We had pressure towards the end of the first half where we had fought our way back into the game after a good start by Scotland. But we failed to capitalise on that situation and then, despite monopolising most of the possession and position in the second half, we failed to put points on the board.

Now, the fact that we failed to kick our penalties was, in retrospect, a mistake. But you have to view that in the overall context of what we have been trying to achieve in English football in the past year.

I appreciate that perhaps you don't want to criticise individuals but, having said that perhaps you should have kicked your penalties, does that call Will Carling's leadership into question?

Well, it's a group thing really. There were some important decisions to be made out on the field and I wouldn't criticise Will because I know just what it is like when you are out there. I've been in a similar situation myself. I can remember back in 1977 as leader of the England side against France. We were having a go at kicking penalties then and to show you how difficult it is when you are out there, we had a kicker who had missed six attempts at goal. We came to something like the seventh attempt and Nigel Horton, the second row man, was screaming at me to do a short penalty move that we practised. But I said no. I called the kicker up and it was a kick that could have won the game for us. He missed, time was up, and we had blown it.

Now at Murrayfield the wind was extremely difficult in the first half and kicking across it like he would have to have done for those penalties from the scrum I've got every sympathy with what happened. Now, in retrospect, we can say, yes he should have kicked them but when you are on the field you just can't believe that things won't go right for you. The team thought they were going to score from that pressure situation.

When, in the second half, Rob Andrew was kicking so sweetly, do you think, again in retrospect, that Mike Teague overdid the picking up and driving around the fringes? Would it not have been more profitable just to have kicked the ball down into that bottom corner?

There is that thought, yes. But you have to go and look a bit deeper than that and look at what we have been trying to achieve. We have been trying to move our game forward and move away from the set-piece stereotypes, you know, just bang and rush, stop the game and then start again with another set-piece. We have been trying to achieve some sort of continuity. We have worked very hard on that and we have worked very hard on getting the players to accept responsibility for what they do on the field and to understand what it is they are trying to do.

DEREK 'STICKS' TURNBULL . . . FROM A HAWICK V HERIOT'S FP MATCH OF FAIRLY RECENT VINTAGE

SCOTLAND V WALES AT MURRAYFIELD IN 1989 . . . GARY ARMSTRONG LOOKS CONCERNED

Now, up until the match at Murrayfield, we had actually been able to do that and a degree of confidence had begun to develop in the side. On the other hand, Scotland had, sort of, muddled through their games. You might call that a slightly biased view from my side but I think it's fair. They had muddled through. They managed to beat the French at Murrayfield, but only after the French had gone a man down; they produced a good win which we've not been able to do at Cardiff and they scraped through to win at Dublin.

By contrast we were all set there to go and were feeling justly confident in what we had achieved. Scotland, however, really didn't have a great deal to lose. They just had to go out and give it their best shot. The underdog in a situation like that will always have a go.

The big disappointment was that it is a situation that England have found themselves in on a number of times over the years and once again we failed in that situation. I make no excuses about that, but that is a source of grief to me at the moment and everybody else involved with the side.

Did you find the atmosphere at Murrayfield intimidating?

It was a fantastic atmosphere, and you could sense that there was something very special in the air. It wasn't intimidating, but there was a certain feeling of déjà vu because, whatever we did, and really if you look at the possession and position that we achieved in the second half, it, almost literally, wasn't going to be our day.

Scotland set the tone right from the outset with that slow march from the tunnel.

That was brilliant. Psychologically that was brilliant, but, you see, that was the home advantage coming into play.

And then we had the singing of 'Flower of Scotland'. I assume that had some kind of effect on the England camp?

Oh yes, it was a whole big lift for the Scots. I know 'Flower of Scotland'. I heard it played at Cardiff and it was as if the band down there had tried to mess things up a bit by putting in a bit of a beat. It is, though, the lament aspect of it that is so important. I think it's a great song. It means a lot to me personally because of the impact it made and the importance it held for the '74 Lions. I know all about 'Flower of Scotland' and the emotive qualities that that song can produce. The environment and the atmosphere were absolutely right at Murrayfield for Scotland to draw on that.

The England props, Probyn and Rendall, looked very tired by the end. You don't think that perhaps the ages of at least four of the front five played a part in your defeat.

Hey listen. These guys have played their socks off. They had had a very demoralising afternoon. They have played the best rugby of their careers throughout the season against all sorts of opposition. They have chewed people up and spat them out the other end. So to knock them after one mediocre performance, and don't forget that we did have the major share of possession and position, is just not on. What was wrong on the day was nothing to do with them. It was our finishing.

If you were to do the whole thing over again is there very much that you would do differently now?

I would hope that our awareness would be that much greater and that we could put the Scots under more pressure. We did try to run the ball at people and we did try to play attractive rugby. All credit to the Scots for stopping us in our endeavours. But it was a little bit disappointing, in some ways, to see the lack of, what's the word I'm looking for, initiative on the part of Scotland.

You know Ian McGeechan extremely well, both from playing days and from the Lions '89 tour to Australia where you were the coaches. You also knew the Scots who had been in the touring party. Did that have any bearing on the match?

Only from the point of view that I know the Scottish players all respected the English players and vice versa from their experience on the tour so there was a lot of mutual respect there on the field. Also there were some guys at Murrayfield really playing their socks off. The likes of JJ (John Jeffrey) wanted to justify himself because of his disappointment at not getting a Test place. Gary Armstrong was another. I was very impressed with Gary. I thought he played with tenacity and commitment and had a great game. It was nice to see him coming through, but, likewise, I didn't expect anything else from someone like Gary. He proved himself to be a terrier out on tour and he was a terrier in the match at Murrayfield.

You are obviously very disappointed, the whole England camp must be. Just how bad was that disappointment on Saturday night after the game?

It is extremely difficult to describe the feeling. I've had some bad sporting experiences in my time as a player, through injury or defeat, but the aftermath of the Grand Slam match has to be the worst experience of my sporting life. Simply because of the weight of expectation and the lack of ability to overcome the problems on the day.

Six days on from the match, have you recovered?

Oh yes. It was a game of football wasn't it. It has taught us one thing. We still have areas of our game that we have to work on despite the fact that we have made great strides. We are now looking forward to going away to play in Italy and then getting a party together for the Argentine tour and then preparing assiduously for what is going to be a demanding 12 months, 18 months really, come the new season. We now have an indication of the areas that we have to pay attention to. We have a rolling programme that will take us to the World Cup (in 1991) but if we had won the Grand Slam on this occasion then we would have thought we were the bee's knees and it might have taken a bit of incentive out of our approach and attitude.

But having been beaten by Scotland has been a severe blow to our pride and I can assure everyone involved in the game that we are not just going to sit down and say, hard luck chaps, well played. We will be back next year with a vengeance.

A BRACE OF SLAMS

The 1925 Match

The *Glasgow Herald* of Monday 23 March 1925, devoted almost an entire page to a report of Scotland's 14-11 victory over England. The match was the first at the new Murrayfield stadium.

SCOTLAND'S RUGBY TRIUMPH

International Championship and Calcutta Cup Won

THRILLING GAME AT MURRAYFIELD

After a tremendously keen encounter Scotland gained a splendid victory over England at Murrayfield on Saturday by 14 points to 11. In consequence the Calcutta Cup, which has not been held by Scotland since 1912, comes north again. By this victory the Scots won outright the International Championship for the first time since 1887. The game — the 47th of the series, of which Scotland has now won 18 to England's 20, with 9 drawn games — marked the opening of the Scottish Union's splendidly arranged new ground, and on that account this inaugural victory is particularly gratifying. The playing pitch was in perfect condition, and a crowd of over 80,000, which must be a record for a Rugby match, witnessed the game. The standard of play may not have been so high as in many previous Internationals, but after the opening passages thrills and excitement abounded. The Scots fully deserved their win, as for quite three-parts of the game they were on the attack, and while the Englishmen as usual showed themselves as clever opportunists, there was a determination about the Scots which ultimately triumphed. Scotland hardly deserved to be three points down at half time, and when she dropped still further behind in the opening minutes of the second period her luck seemed to have deserted her. A strong rally, however, saw

127

the lead reduced to one point, thanks to a resolutely taken score by A. C. Wallace and a wonderful goal-kick from the touch line by A. C. Gillies. From this point onwards excitement was at fever heat. The Scots were continually on the attack, but somehow chance after chance went wrong. J. B. Nelson had a couple of likely runs checked on the line, and then G. G. Aitken had the ill luck to kick the ball against one of the goal posts for the ball to rebound into play, when the English defence was well beaten, and then H. Waddell narrowly failed with a drop at goal. Scotland's luck seemed dead out. Then another chance for a drop goal came Waddell's way, and this time he made sure with a well-judged kick, and with five minutes left for play Scotland led by three points. In spite of desperate attempts by England to save the game the Scots, slightly favoured by fortune, maintained their lead, and the game was won.

Scotland's Fine Forwards

A large part of the credit for the victory must be given to the Scottish forwards, all of whom played with great determination and energy. Though manifestly at a disadvantage as regards height and weight, the Scots stuck manfully to the opponents, and had considerably the better of them in the tight scrummages and the loose dribbling. Their heeling, too, was better than that of the Englishmen. J. M. Bannerman was at the top of his form all through, and some of his efforts to score — particularly one at the close of the first half — were very fine. His tackling, in common with that of the others was very sound. J. W. Scott was particularly prominent in the loose, and his height again stood them in good stead at the line-out. J. R. Paterson made his best appearance in an International match, being never far off the ball, while all the others played their parts in the struggle with great determination. A. C. Gillies, if not quite so prominent as in some of his previous games, deserves special credit for his wonderful goal-kick, which reduced Scotland's deficit to a single point. The English forwards hardly came up to expectations in the fight, but where they had an advantage was at the line-out, where they backed up the man with the ball with great quickness and intelligence. Their wide, swinging passes also were dangerous, and they all showed a fine sense of position. A serious blemish in their play, however, was their tendency to offside and obstructional tactics, while two of them at least were guilty of distinctly unfair and dangerous play. It is a great pity that such fine players should have to employ such tactics, and it is certainly not the sort of thing one expects from International players. W. W. Wakefield gave the pack a splendid lead, and his try at the commencement of the second half from a cross kick by L. J. Corbett was nicely judged. A. T. Voyce was hardly so much in evidence as a winger as last season, but he was in the right place for combination with his backs when R. Hamilton-Wickes

SCOTLAND'S GRAND SLAM SIDE OF 1925. THE TEAM WHICH PLAYED ENGLAND IN THE DECIDING GAME OF THE SEASON AT THE NEW MURRAYFIELD. JIMMY IRELAND IS FOURTH FROM THE RIGHT IN THE BACK ROW
BACK ROW: D. J. MacMYN (CAMBRIDGE UNIVERSITY), J. W. SCOTT (STEWART'S COLLEGE FP), A. C. GILLIES (WATSONIANS AND CARLISLE), J. C. H. IRELAND (GLASGOW HIGH SCHOOL FP), R. A. HOWIE (KIRKCALDY), I. S. SMITH (OXFORD UNIVERSITY)
FRONT ROW: G. G. AITKEN (OXFORD UNIVERSITY), D. S. DAVIES (HAWICK), J. M. BANNERMAN (GLASGOW HIGH SCHOOL FP), G. P. S. MacPHERSON (OXFORD UNIVERSITY) CAPTAIN, D. DRYSDALE (HERIOT'S FP), A. C. WALLACE (OXFORD UNIVERSITY), H. WADDELL (GLASGOW ACADEMICALS)
SEATED: J. B. NELSON (GLASGOW ACADEMICALS), J. R. PETERSON (BIRKENHEAD PARK)

scored just before half-time. Of the rest W. G. Luddington was most noticeable, but several of the English pack were showing signs of distress well before the finish.

The Halves

The Glasgow Academical half-back pair, J. B. Nelson and H. Waddell, had a large say in the game, and, indeed, half of Scotland's points came from them. Nelson very cleverly took the chance provided by G. P. E. Macpherson for Scotland's first score, and in defence he performed as usual with pluck. In his service from the scrum he did not always display accuracy, but the quick breaking up of the English forwards probably accounted for this. He had, in addition to his score, one or two other fine efforts in the second half. H. Waddell played soundly if not quite so brilliantly as he has done and his coolness in his second attempt at dropping for goal was very marked. His defence, bar one unlucky lapse which led to England's second try, was sound, and he kicked well. The English pair were not so successful, but E. J. Massey had not too many chances of showing his abilities as a scrum worker afforded him by his forwards. He was very quick, however, in spoiling tactics. E. Myers at stand-off overdid the kick ahead, but tackled very soundly.

Scottish Three-Quarters Disappoint

In the three-quarter line, where much was expected of the Oxford quartet, things did not go nearly so well as had been anticipated. For this state of affairs the centres, G. G. Aitken and G. P. S. Macpherson, must be blamed. While doing well in tackling, both tried to cut through far too often, and were time and again downed by the English centres. In view of the keen marking and tackling of the Englishmen, it might have paid better to have tried a kick ahead or a quick pass on to the wings. Macpherson, however, must be given great credit for the opening he made for Scotland's first score. I. S. Smith got only one real chance to show his attacking powers, and was rather unsteady in his defence. A. C. Wallace did very well on the other wing, and took his chances cleverly, though on at least one occasion he dropped his pass when in a favourable position. As a line the Scottish three-quarters were a more dangerous quartet than the Englishmen who preferred to concentrate on defence rather than attack. There was, however, a falling-off in their combined play from that shown against Wales and Ireland. The English threes were a thoroughly sound line in defence, and their keen marking and deadly tackling upset the Scots' attack. H. M. Locke and L. J. Corbett in the centre were particularly strong in this respect, as Macpherson and Aitken well knew, and Corbett's kicking was also most useful. R. Hamilton-Wickes showed cleverness in attack and ran strongly for his score, but the game ran less to A. M. Smallwood's wing. He looked after Wallace fairly well, but was at fault when the latter got over for Scotland's second score. The English three-quarters evidently felt the handicap of being slower than their opponents, and it was perhaps due to this that they did so much kicking down the centre of the field to their forwards, who were usually in position for this move. D. Drysdale at full-back for Scotland played up to his reputation. Save for being at fault when Hamilton-Wickes got past him, his play was without mistake. His lengthy kicks to touch from mark or penalty kick gained ground again and again for his side. The English full-back, T. E. Holliday, did fairly well, but his kicking lacked length, and was not always accurate. He was badly at fault in not stopping Nelson when he scored, allowing himself to be handed off very simply. There was a wonderful scene at the finish, many of the crowd swarming on to the field, so that the players had to make their way to the dressing-rooms through a delighted and cheering crowd.

SCOTLAND WINS

GREAT SECOND-HALF RECOVERY

DROP GOAL VICTORY

Scotland 14 Points : England 11 Points

The new ground of the Scottish Rugby Union at Murrayfield was opened on Saturday, when a crowd of some 60,000 witnessed the first post-war defeat of England by Scotland. Teams:

SCOTLAND

Back — D. Drysdale (Heriot's F.P.'s)

Three-quarters — Ian S. Smith (Oxford University), G. P. S. Macpherson (Oxford University), G. G. Aitken (Oxford University), and A. C. Wallace (Oxford University).

Half-backs — H. Waddell and T. B. Nelson (Glasgow Academicals).

Forwards — J. M. Bannerman (Glasgow High School F.P.'s), D. S. Davies (Hawick), R. Howie (Kirkcaldy), J. C. H. Ireland (Glasgow High School F.P.'s), D. J. MacMyn (Cambridge University), J. W. Scott (Stewart's College F.P.'s), A. C. Gillies (Watsonians), and J. R. Paterson (Birkenhead Park).

ENGLAND

Back — T. E. Holliday (Aspatria).

Three-quarters — R. H. Hamilton-Wickes (Harlequins), L. J. Corbett (Bristol), H. M. Locke (Birkenhead Park), and A. M. Smallwood (Leicester).

Half-backs — E. Myers (Bradford) and E. J. Massey (Leicester).

Forwards — W. W. Wakefield (Harlequins), R. Cove-Smith (Old Merchant Taylors), A. F. Blakiston (Liverpool), J. S. Tucker (Bristol), W. G. E. Luddington (Devonport Services), R. R. F. Maclennan (Old Merchant Taylors), A. T. Voyce (Gloucester), and D. Cumming (Cambridge University).

Referee — Mr A. E. Freethy (Neath).

THE GAME

Scotland carried the first scrum, and Nelson slung out to Aitken, who found touch in the English half. Drysdale further improved Scotland's position with a free kick that followed three minutes later, the Heriotonian showing right away that he was in his most effective kicking form. So far England had had no chance of settling down, and a free kick brought them but little relief, Wallace returning the ball to Holliday with a powerful punt. It was a trifle too strong, however, and the Englishman touched down without any embarrassment. When Macpherson got his first chance he made good use of it but his parting pass to Smith miscarried. A similar move three minutes later brought a similar disappointment and Nelson, when he tried, had no better luck. This time, Locke picked up smartly, and, finding the Scottish defence out of position, reached Drysdale ten yards from the home line before he was stopped.

THE FIRST SCORE

In the scrum that followed a Scottish forward was penalised for offside, and Luddington from a difficult angle kicked a perfect goal — the first score at Murrayfield. In the Scots' reply to this unexpected reverse Drysdale was again the outstanding figure, long-carrying punts to touch keeping the visitors confined within their own '25'. Here our forwards got going spiritedly, but the English defence stood up to them pluckily, and at length Myers cleared with a judicious kick to touch. Two more free kicks against England, with which Drysdale again made valuable ground, showed up the visitors' scrum tactics in an unfavourable light, but this was soon forgotten when, five minutes later, Scotland scored what proved to be the best try of the game. Macpherson deserves much of the credit for it, for it was style. The ball passed through half a dozen hands before the movement came to a stop in the home '25'. A kick to touch saved the situation, but a few minutes later a miss by Aitken almost let Corbett in, Davies by a fine effort coming to the rescue by throwing himself on the ball.

ENGLAND'S HALF-TIME LEAD

England at this stage was playing hard for a score, and it came just before half-time as the culmination of a clever passing movement between Voyce — who was as much three-quarter as forward — and Hamilton-Wickes. The Harlequin was grassed after having crossed the line, but he got to his feet again and ran on to touch down behind the posts, Luddington converting with the easy kick.

Half-time score — England 8 points, Scotland 5 points.

Scarcely had play been resumed when Cove-Smith incurred the displeasure of the crowd by an uncalled-for scrum infringement. This, and the incident which led up to the injury suffered by Drysdale in the closing minutes — Blakiston was the offender here — were, it may be said, the only discreditable passages in the game. Within ten minutes England found themselves in the enjoyment of a bigger lead, thanks as much to weak Scottish defences as to English enterprise. Corbett, taking advantage of an opening, made for the corner, but when faced by Smith cross-kicked to the Scottish goal. Here Waddell failed to gather the ball on the line, and Wakefield, seeing his chance, promptly darted over and secured the touch. Luddington prepared to take the kick, but through some misunderstanding he allowed the Scottish forwards to come right up to the place and tap the ball away without making any advance himself.

GILLIES FINE KICK

This 'let-off' for the Scots seemed to brace them up somewhat, for on their next visit to Holliday, a score came. Wallace running resolutely for the corner and touching down just before being thrown into touch — along with the flag. The kick was a most difficult one, requiring both long carry and accurate direction, but Gillies found the mark all right. Only one point down now, the Scots attacked with more determination than ever, and for some 20 minutes dominated the play. MacMyn on one occasion threw away a good chance by passing forward when Wallace was unmarked. Scott, with four or five forwards in support, broke away from his own half and beat Holliday, only to find Smallwood cut across and save daringly. Macpherson and Aitken tried time and again to cut through, but always found themselves well marked. Smith, with the only chance of the game that came his way, ran determinedly, but was pulled down ten yards from the line. Waddell dropped a goal, but it was disallowed. In a word, Scotland did everything but score.

WADDELL'S DROP GOAL

At long last, however, the lead changed hands, Waddell, with commendable coolness in a nerve-trying situation, dropping a goal from the '25' line. In the five minutes' play that remained England made a desperate effort to save the game. First Smallwood broke away cleverly, only to be stopped by Drysdale. Then Myers tried to hurl himself over the line, but found himself downed immediately. Finally Corbett got right through, only to fall through sheer exhaustion when another yard would have carried him over. It was in the melee that followed this incident that Drysdale was kicked on the head and badly stunned. However, he stuck to his post to the end, and when the whistle sounded was singled out for special attention by the crowd of delighted enthusiasts that swarmed on to the field and mobbed the victors. Before this, however, Holliday, with practically the last kick of the game, had almost given England victory with a drop kick from long range, the ball passing narrowly outside.

THE INTERNATIONAL CHAMPIONSHIP

	P	W	D	L	F	A	Pts
Scotland	4	4	0	0	77	37	8
Ireland	4	2	1	1	42	26	5
England	3	1	1	1	29	30	3
Wales	4	1	3	0	34	60	2
France	3	0	3	0	12	45	0

The 1984 Match

(From the Glasgow Herald *of 19 March 1984)*

SCOTLAND ARE THE CHAMPIONS AFTER ANOTHER DAMNED CLOSE-RUN THING

BY BILL McMURTRIE

Scotland 21: France 12

IN THE CATHEDRAL of Scottish rugby, as the massed choirs raised their victory anthem and the golden banners unfurled with their rampant lions, the game's honours returned to Caledonia after an absence that has been too long. Scotland became Grand Slam champions with their victory over France at Murrayfield on Saturday.

Not since 1938 had Scotland been outright holders of the international championship. Not since 1925, the only time in the past, had they beaten the four other countries in one championship campaign.

Now, over the coming year, rugby Scots, wherever they go, whatever the occasion, whoever they are, will walk taller and more spritely. It is a glorious feeling to follow the best team in Western Europe and record their deeds.

Scotland's victory, warming hearts on a chilly afternoon, was a result of perseverance, discipline, courage, and character. Most of those qualities were needed to confine the French first-half pressure to just a 6-3 lead, and all showed through together as the Scots edged finally ahead in the last ten minutes.

Twice in the second half the Scots drew themselves level, and on the first occasion they were immediately knocked back, with Jean-Patrick Lescarboura striking over a towering drop goal from fully 40 metres. Such a score might have finished some teams, but not these Scots. They pressed, their game restored after first-half difficulties, and it was the French who cracked.

Scotland's ready reply to Lescarboura's drop goal was for Peter Dods to hoist a high kick on the left, and the full-back's vigorous follow-up was such that he caught the unprotected Serge Blanco with no chance to clear. The Scottish forwards swarmed in behind Dods, and together they carried Blanco almost over the goal-line, his feet seeming barely to touch the ground.

Nothing came directly of that. The Scots, however, had made their point, and soon Dods notched the equalising points with his fourth penalty goal, when Jean-Charles Orso was offside in stopping a thrust by Keith Robertson, John Rutherford, and the inevitable David Leslie.

135

Three minutes later the lead was regained after a deep diagonal kick by Rutherford to the left. Pierre Berbizier, threatened by the chasing David Johnston and Roger Baird, sliced his clearance, and from the throw-in by Colin Deans to the tail Joinel tapped down for Jim Calder to dive through unopposed for the try.

Dods converted and added his fifth penalty goal in injury time after he had been felled by Blanco, late and brutally. The French full-back jumped at Dods, attempting to block the Scot's kick from his own ten-metre line, and when the Gala lad had recovered from the heavy knock on the head from Blanco's legs he struck the kick over from no more than 24 metres range.

Dods scored 17 points in the Royal Bank international and exactly 50 in the championship. The first of those figures equalled Andy Irvine's record for a Scottish international, the second eclipsed the previous best by a Scot in a championship season, 35 by Irvine four years ago, and overall Dods has scored 98 points in just nine games for his country. Irvine made 273 in 51. Lescarboura also had a half-century of points in the championship. His 54 with eight against Scotland, beat Ollie Campbell's championship record of 52, set last season.

Quite apart from the mere statistics, Dods exacted a heavy penalty on French indiscretions. Over the match the visitors were penalised 18 times, more than twice the figure against the disciplined Scots, and the difference might even have been greater and the consequent margin even wider if the referee, Winston Jones, making his international début, had been more strict in the first hour against the French persistence in going over the ball in the tackle.

It was only in the last quarter that Jones stamped down on that form of offside, and so disconcerted were the French by it that even Jean-Pierre Rives lost his cool. Scotland, by comparison, kept their heads even under the most severe pressure in the first half after the Gala full-back's first penalty goal in only the third minute.

France responded to that score with a sustained seige on the Scottish line, the main weaponry being Jean-Luc Joinel's drives, Jerome Gallion's probing, and Lescarboura's punting. Jim Pollock was twice forced to concede five-metre scrums, Patrick Sella's pass eluded Jacques Begu when a try was on in the right corner, Joinel lost it in driving over the line, and it was only after 23 minutes that the Scots eventually cracked, though just the once.

It was one of those scores most difficult to defend against, with Orso picking up from the back of a scrum on the Scottish line and putting Gallion over on the narrow side for his third try in four championship matches this season. Lescarboura converted, but such was the Scottish discipline that it was only after that try that they were penalised for the first time in the match.

To concede only one try in that first half was a commentary on the Scots in defence. Their tackling was mainly secure and, just as important, Leslie was supreme in gathering in the ball on the ground. No Frenchman could touch him in that respect.

Scotland played the first half knowing that they were up against the most physical team in the championship. However, they had the courage to stand up to it to a man, and in the few minutes before the interval they struck back.

Leslie and Calder were the principals, the former twice standing off from scrums to drive at the opposition, the spearhead for others to lance the French defence.

All that gave hope that the Scots might just lift their low-key game. For too long in the first half they lacked the quality possession to break the French grip.

Iain Milne, as much as any, however, maintained his personal standard throughout in the scrummage, and the pack refused to submit to the French attempts to compress the lineout. Indeed, the latter tactic probably helped Scotland's eventual try: the French concentrated too much on the jumper and left the hole for Calder to dive through.

Milne's persistence, too, paid off. Scotland's scrummage came again, so much so that midway in the second half the home pack drove over one French put-in and also disintegrated the opposition on the line. Only a penalty against Scotland there denied Paxton a try.

Milne and Dods had the most obvious mementoes of a physical game. Milne had a blackened right eye, and the same side of the Gala full-back's face was swollen, the eye almost completely closed in the early part of the match.

All that was part of the character that has shone through in the Scottish team. They have faith in themselves, they react to Jim Aitken's demands, and they have unremitting commitment, exemplified by Leslie, no more so than when he and Gallion chased back for a long French throw-in. Their courses were programmed for collision, neither holding back, and the clash knocked Gallion cold. The French scrum-half had to be carried off on a stretcher.

As soon as Berbizier arrived as replacement, Lescarboura added a penalty goal, but by then the Scottish forwards had raised their game all round, even though they were denied much ruck ball because of the French insistence on falling offside over the ball. Scotland's scrummage responded to Milne's example, and in the lineout Alister Campbell, Alan Tomes, Paxton and Leslie resisted the French.

Because of the quality of the French defence at close quarters the Scots were unable to develop a game off the back row and Roy Laidlaw. Rutherford, however, had found the line and length in his kicking that had been missing in the first half, and the worries of half-time were transformed.

Two penalty goals by Dods inside as many minutes drew the score to 9-all and despite Lescarboura's long drop goal, the match was swinging in Scotland's favour. That feeling turned to fact with the fourth Dods penalty goal and Calder's try, and a famous victory was won, even if, like Waterloo, it was a damned close run thing.

SCOTLAND

P. W. Dods (*Gala*), J. A. Pollock (*Gosforth*), K. W. Robertson (*Melrose*), D. I. Johnston (*Watsonians*), G. R. T. Baird (*Kelso*), J. Y. Rutherford (*Selkirk*), R. J. Laidlaw (*Jed-Forest*), J. Aitken (*Gala*) captain, C. T. Deans (*Hawick*), I. G. Milne (*Heriot's FP*), A. J. Campbell (*Hawick*), A. J. Tomes (*Hawick*), J. H. Calder (*Stewart's-Melville FP*), I. A. M. Paxton (*Selkirk*), D. G. Leslie (*Gala*).

'THE TURNING POINT.' RONNIE BROWNE OF THE CORRIES' EVOCATIVE ROYAL BANK WATERCOLOUR OF JIM CALDER'S CRUCIAL TRY DURING THE 1984 GRAND SLAM DECIDER AGAINST FRANCE. ANOTHER VERSION, FOR THE 1990 SIDE, IS PROMISED

MEMBERS OF THE 1984 GRAND SLAM SQUAD WITH SOME OF THE SPOILS OF VICTORY

FRANCE

S. Blanco (*Biarritz*), J. Begu (*Dax*), P. Sella (*Agen*), D. Codorniou (*Narbonne*), P. Esteve (*Narbonne*), J. P. Lescarboura (*Dax*), J. Gallion (*Toulon*), P. Dospital (*Bayonne*), P. Dintrans (*Tarbes*), D. Dubroca (*Agen*), P. Haget (*Biarritz*), J. Condom (*Boucan*), J.-P. Rives (*Racing Club*) captain, J. C. Orso (*Nice*), J. L. Joinel (*Brive*). Replacement — P. Berbizier (*Lourdes*) for Gallion (60 minutes).

Referee — W. Jones (Wales).

Irvine bows out of international arena

ANDY IRVINE yesterday informed Colin Telfer, who will coach the party for the forthcoming tour of Romania, that he will not be available. Nor does he intend to play representative rugby, at district or international level, in the future.

Thirty-three in September, and a married man with two children, Irvine, a partner in a firm of chartered surveyors, has 51 caps and is, along with his old comrade-in-arms, Jim Renwick of Hawick, the most capped Scot.

A replacement against both Ireland and France, the former Scottish captain came so close to a 52nd cap having been sent to the back pitch at Murrayfield to warm up when Peter Dods and Roger Baird were injured in Saturday's bruising Grand Slam encounter with France. He confessed that he experienced an eagerness and a tingle of expectation at the prospect of getting on to the field which he had not known for close on two years.

The recipient at the post-match dinner of a warm tribute from Jean-Pierre Rives for his contribution to world rugby, and also of a plaque from the French Barbarians, Irvine had, in fact, looked forward to having a real go at getting back to full fitness and form this winter.

Alas, his season was bedevilled by injury from early September and that sequence of misfortune blunted his appetite.

'We had the will, the wish, the chance, and the team to do it'

'WE DESERVE TO BE WHERE WE ARE!' That was how Jim Aitken, Scotland's captain, summed up his country's Grand Slam triumph at the dinner after the international in which his team had beaten France by 21-12 at Murrayfield on Saturday. No one could deny him the right to say it when Scotland had waited 59 years since their only previous clean sweep through the international championship.

Aitken, now unbeaten in six internationals as captain, was, however, quick to record his gratitude to Jim Telfer, Scotland's coach. 'If anyone owes anything to anyone, it is the players who owe a lot to you, Jim,' the captain said.

140

Ian MacGregor, convenor of the Scottish selectors, also had sincere thanks for the coach after the match. 'Jim had the will to do it, the wish to do it, the chance to do it, and the team to do it.'

Telfer described himself as 'a happy man after the trials and tribulations in New Zealand.' Just last year he was coach of the Lions who were subjected to a whitewash by the All Blacks in the four Test matches.

All agreed that the victory over France was close, even though the final margin was nine points. 'At half-time I was a worried man,' Aitken remarked. 'We knew what we wanted to do in the first half, but we just couldn't do it. We weren't able to get quality ball. The French were getting it, but fortunately we were defending well and tackling well.

'At 9-9 I thought we were back in the game. I could feel a difference in the team.'

It was then that Jean-Patrick Lescarboura restored France to the lead with a huge drop goal from all of 40 metres. 'That could have knocked the stuffing out of us,' Aitken commented, 'but we did the right thing. We got back into their half and kept working away.'

MacGregor described it as a victory of character. 'We were down, struggling, and beginning to get a wee bit bewildered, but in the end the character came through,' he said.

Telfer commented: 'We assumed that the game against France would be like the games against the British teams, but they were a league better than that. That's why we didn't get started until the second half.

'I thought they were very physical, and a good side in the first 40 minutes, when they really turned it on. They were playing to the top of their form, and we just hung on. We were fortunate to turn just three points down. The players deserve credit for coming back in the second half.

'The turning point for me was at 12-12 when Blanco was caught under a high ball and we carried him for 25 yards. I've never seen that before, and we scored immediately after that.

'I would commend our scrum, particularly Iain Milne. I thought towards the end France cracked up and disintegrated.'

Scots almost lost
record breaker

PETER DODS was close to being replaced early on in Scotland's match against France at Murrayfield on Saturday. But he stayed on and kicked 17 points in helping Scotland to a 21-12 victory to take the championship and complete the Grand Slam for the first time since 1925.

After Dods had given the Scots the lead with a penalty goal in three minutes his right eye was almost completely closed in a collision. 'It was fuzzy for a while,' the Gala full-back admitted afterwards, 'but I got used to it and although I missed a couple of kicks, things worked out right in the end.'

'I was a wee bit worried when Peter missed the two kicks,' Jim Aitken, Scotland's captain, said. 'But he reckoned he'd shaken it off, and he did come again. I think we were right to keep him kicking.'

With his 17 points, Dods equalled Andy Irvine's record for a Scot in an international match, and he also took his season's championship total to 50. That beat Irvine's previous Scottish record set four years ago.

Iain Milne, Scotland's tight-head prop, also finished the game with a battered right eye, and Jerome Gallion, the French scrum-half, spent Saturday night in hospital after having been laid out in a collision with David Leslie.

Chapter Eight

TWENTY-TWO OF THE BEST
The Players

By DAVID STEELE

DAVID SOLE: *prop and captain*
Full name: *David Michael Barclay Sole*
Born: *8 May 1962, Aylesbury*
Height: *5ft. 11in.*
Weight: *16st. 4lb.*
Caps: *25, first against France, 1986*
Club: *Edinburgh Academicals*
Education: *Blairmore, Glenalmond, Exeter University*
Occupation: *grain buyer*
Married: *to Jane, with one-year-old son, Jamie, and second child due in*
    September

Trying to single out one great moment from his greatest season proves impossible for the Grand Slam captain. Instead, the second player to lead a side into the history books from the formerly unglamorous position of prop-forward chooses a few from the many 'firsts' of his remarkable season. 'I would have to say that winning away from home for the first time in my career at Dublin, was a great feeling. Then going on to win at Cardiff and achieving the result we did at Murrayfield was just fantastic.' Sole, somewhat enigmatically, says that he was 'not surprised . . . but did not expect it' when the captaincy was offered to him last autumn in the place of the resting Finlay Calder. He had some experience of the responsibility, having captained Bath and the Anglo Scots, led the Barbarians against the All Blacks and worn the mantle of British Lions captain on two occasions in Australia last summer. He emerged after Jim Aitken, the 1984 Grand Slam captain, had gone off into the international wilderness and Gerry McGuinness had been tried at loose-head for a season and a bit. Sole, now reckoned world class, has come in for criticism from the Luddites of the front-row society but has won many friends for his speed and agility around the paddock — and his scrummaging has also come on a long, long way.

Sole puts the success of his Grand Slam team down to the spirit which exists in the camp. He calls it, rather surprisingly when one sees those bandaged and marauding forwards, 'a family atmosphere' and points to the fact that, despite injury, the spare full-back, Peter Dods, remained part of the squad, spent most of Saturday with the team and attended the dinner in the evening. 'This is the kind of spirit which has meant so much to us this season. We played to our strengths and as each win came along it came as a bonus. At no time did we start thinking silly thoughts about Grand Slams and championships until it was firmly in our grasp,' says Sole.

He praises the inter-district championship as being a good way for players with international aspirations, to keep up a high level of performance and also to get to know one another. But above all he pays tribute to the unsung heroes of Scottish rugby — 'the guys who have 20 or 30 caps and never had a crack at a Grand Slam' — for the influence they have had on the game. He is reluctant to single out individuals but, when pressed, mentions John Beattie. The description of 'hard

man' is meant in the nicest possible way and he regrets that Beattie was unable, because of injury, to continue his international career.

That is the last time we will hear of anyone being singled out by the man who, with his superb athleticism, has laid the ghost of Neanderthal-man-as-prop-forward to rest. Instead, he responds to the question of where his influence has come from thus: 'It has come from people like the Scottish coaches, Finlay Calder, JJ, Iain Milne . . .' Were a halt not called, he would go on, this Grand Slam captain who, rather than fussing about his place in history, has one clear message for rugby enthusiasts everywhere: 'Rugby must be about enjoyment. That is what we have done this season, enjoyed ourselves. Success and enjoyment are inexorably linked but the most important at all times must be enjoyment.'

KENNETH MILNE: *booker*
Full name: *Kenneth Stuart Milne*
Born: *1 December 1961, Edinburgh*
Height: *6ft.*
Weight: *14st. 3lb.*
Caps: *ten, first against Wales, 1989*
Club: *Heriot's FP*
Education: *George Heriot's School, Stevenson College*
Occupation: *sales representative*
Married: *to Eleanor*

In common with a couple of his fellow players, Kenny Milne sees no one moment as sticking out above all others in the Grand Slam season. Instead, the gradual build-up of the squad's performance and confidence and that final killer blow against England will be his memories of the historic 1989-90 season.

It was all the more fitting perhaps that he shared in such glory in the centenary season of Heriot's FP, the club he — along with brothers, Iain and David, known together as the 'Three Bears' of modern rugby folklore — has served so well. Unfortunately for them they could not secure the championship which was so deservedly won by Melrose but Kenny has had a great season, nonetheless. He says: 'I have thoroughly enjoyed the season and the final result was just fantastic.'

Kenny admits, with no offence meant to Paul Burnell and doubtless none taken, that he misses having brother Iain under his right oxter when packing down for Scotland these days. 'I do miss Iain as he is a great scrummager and a great player, but we have done well as a front row losing no strikes against the head that I can recall and even pinching a few for ourselves.'

For Kenny, as for the bulk of the players, Scotland honour, added to Grand Slam fame, had led to enormous demands on his time. He echoes the words of every player when he pays tribute to his employer for the time and patience afforded him when rugby duties call.

'I am making my début speech soon at an FP rugby club and if that goes well I'll have a go at a few more. In the meantime I'll stick to doing a bit of coaching for the youngsters at various clubs. That way I can just shout at them and don't have to think up any clever stories.'

PAUL BURNELL: *prop*
Full name: *Andrew Paul Burnell*
Born: *29 September 1965, Edinburgh*
Height: *6ft.*
Weight: *16st. 2lb.*
Caps: *nine, first against England, 1989*
Club: *London Scottish*
Education: *Blue Coat School, Reading, and Leicester University*
Occupation: *sales representative*
Married: *no*

The formidable figure of 'The Bear', alias Iain Milne of Heriot's and Scotland, breathing down the neck would be enough to concentrate anyone's mind — none more so than the 24-year-old Anglo-Scot prop who took his place in the international team. Paul Burnell is the first, however, to dismiss any suggestion of bitterness between him and the man whose tight-head berth he stepped into when injury and loss of form eased Iain Milne aside from international reckoning. 'I have always felt the presence of ''The Bear'' around since I was first capped as he is a superb player and is a credit to any team he plays for. I have been fortunate enough that the selectors have had faith in me and I have managed to keep my place. I hope I have justified that faith and feel that my game has been going well over the past couple of seasons.'

He reluctantly admits that his mobility and ability to tackle even the speed merchants has added a useful dimension to the forward play and says: 'You may not see me running around mad with the ball the way David Sole does but hopefully I am not too far behind.' He adds: 'There is no animosity between Iain and me. I am good friends with Kenny Milne and I see Iain from time to time and we talk a lot about each other's game. We will be touring together so I will have to be at my best to keep him from taking back the No 3 shirt which I do not plan to let go easily.'

Paul had a season with Leicester University, then with the famous 'Tigers' of Leicester before the travelling from Reading became too much and he opted for London Scottish from whence many a famous cap has come. It is a tradition he is happy to maintain and hopes that he has much more to offer to his country.

'Quite simply it has been a great honour to be involved in this whole thing.'

PAUL BURNELL

CHRIS GRAY: *lock*
Full name: *Christopher Anthony Gray*
Born: *11 July 1960, Haddington*
Height: *6ft. 5in.*
Weight: *16st. 12lb.*
Caps: *ten, first against Wales, 1989*
Club: *Nottingham*
Education: *Gordonstoun, Edinburgh Academy, Edinburgh University*
Occupation: *dental surgeon*
Married: *no*

The amiable giant, dentist Chris Gray, was beginning to feel the aches and pains of an unbelievably punishing season as captain of Nottingham and part of the highly mobile Scottish 'boiler house'. He is brutally frank when he talks of the failure of himself and Damian Cronin to 'produce the goods' against Ireland early in February. 'Neither of us played well that day and knew we would have to do better or we would be letting down the rest of the team and the best supporters in the world.'

Chris is reluctant to go into detail for fear that such delicate intelligence may fall into the hands of an unfriendly power but admits: 'The work done by the coaches, by the rest of the pack and by us on lineout play was immense. We worked, worked again and worked some more on ringing the changes and produced results which speak for themselves. We managed to make the supposedly top-line out-men in the championship look ordinary and that took team-work.'

DAMIAN CRONIN: *lock*
Full name: *Damian Francis Cronin*
Born: *17 April 1963, West Germany*
Height: *6ft. 6in.*
Weight: *16st. 8lb.*
Caps: *15, first against Ireland, 1988*
Club: *Bath*
Education: *Campion School, Essex, Prior Park College, Essex*
Occupation: *sales manager*
Married: *no*

The feeling of elation at the moment the Grand Slam was secured will live with the big Anglo Scot for ever. 'I felt about 30 feet tall. I have never known a feeling of excitement and relief like it,' he says.

The Bath lock-forward arrived on the international scene in 1988 after a happenstance encounter with David Sole, his Bath club-mate and then captain of the Anglo Scots. The pair were chatting in the restaurant where Damian, then yet to emerge as a first XV player at Bath, worked and David was bemoaning the fact that Chris Gray had called off from the Anglos' game against Glasgow. He inquired, half-joking, if the big fellow had any Scottish blood and, when the reply came that his mum was from Musselburgh, David exclaimed: 'That'll do for me' and headed off to contact the committee.

Some still indulge in the odd mickey-take of Damian's cultured home-counties accent but his six-and-a-half-foot, 16-stone-plus frame usually deters most. Indeed, he insists: 'I was singing ''Flower of Scotland'' just about the loudest in the dressing-room after the match. I don't know how it sounds with this accent of mine but I was belting it out with the best of them.'

He was disappointed with last year's tour of Japan where 'nothing went right in the one and only Test' but is looking forward with eager anticipation to his 'first and biggest rugby Test overseas' when he joins the squad for New Zealand.

Like his second-row partner, Chris Gray, Damian concedes that things did not start well around the lineout in the Grand Slam season. 'We were coming in for a bit of stick but hopefully with all the hard work that was done we answered all the critics.' Despite his insistence that the jump for joy at the final whistle is the lasting memory of the season, he will quietly admit that he really rather enjoyed that try against the Welsh at Cardiff when his rapid follow-up and inexorable charge to the line led to the Scots advantage and ultimate victory. 'Those away wins were just as important to us, if not more so, than the games at Murrayfield. Without them there would have been nothing.'

JOHN JEFFREY: *flanker*
Full name: *John Jeffrey*
Born: *25 March 1959, Kelso*
Height: *6ft. 4in.*
Weight: *14st. 5lb.*
Caps: *28, first against Australia, 1984*
Club: *Kelso*
Education: *Merchiston Castle School, Newcastle University*
Occupation: *farmer*
Married: *no*

The 'White Shark' thought for a moment or two before nominating his favourite moment of a momentous rugby season. 'The walk out of the Murrayfield tunnel into that cauldron of noise. I have never experienced anything like it.'

JJ, as he is universally and affectionately known, recalls a telephone conversation with David Sole about the slow march out of the tunnel. 'David recalled Gary Callander leading a trial side out at Murrayfield at walking pace and thought that would be a good idea for Saturday. I thought it would work and the rest of the players agreed without hesitation. It gave us a chance to soak up that fabulous atmosphere which I believe brought out a little bit more from every man in the side. It would be a strange man who was not already psyched up for a game like this but this made it even better.'

Only the foolish raise the question of a certain incident involving JJ, England's No 8 Dean Richards and the Calcutta Cup in 1988 and, indeed, when Terry Wogan, no less, said he was not going to bring it up on his chat show, he was rewarded with that broad smile and the response: 'Good' and the unspoken suggestion that the next question might be in order.

The superlatives run out when one tries to chronicle the part that the Kelso club's most-capped player and the current team's senior man in terms of international appearances has played in the recent success of Scotland. Yet he points out: 'I am really glad that Derek White was with us for the whole season up until that knock in the Grand Slam match and that he will be in New Zealand because we are short of cover when it comes to a genuine No 8.'

He laughs when it is pointed out that the man who switched across to the back of the scrummage after 27 minutes against England — JJ in his usual club position — did not do such a bad job and responds: 'Aye, he came on to a bit of a game.'

His response to the news that the 'ultimate wind-up' is to be recorded forever between these covers is another hearty laugh and the comment: 'It was a cracker, I fell for it hook, line and sinker and the fact that they all kept it going until the next morning on the bus to training made it all the more painful. But I had a laugh to go with my very red face.'

He is quite sure that all the hype worked against England and favoured Scotland. 'In every interview the senior players gave — and we were the only ones

154

dealing with the press — we went along with the fact that we really had no chance. Deep down, though, we knew that odds like those offered were ludicrous in a two-horse race and that led to a burst of pride and commitment the likes of which I have never seen before. It was superb.'

FINLAY CALDER: *flanker*
Full name: *Finlay Calder*
Born: *20 August 1957, Haddington*
Height: *6ft. 2in.*
Weight: *15st. 6lb.*
Caps: *26, first against France, 1986*

Club: *Stewart's-Melville FP*
Education: *Daniel Stewart's and Melville College*
Occupation: *grain shipper*
Married: *to Liz, with six-year-old son, David and daughter, Hazel, four*

There will be a huge gap to fill in Scottish international rugby when Finlay Calder finishes his phenomenal career after the summer tour of New Zealand. The younger of the Calder twins — some two hours younger than brother Jim whose try against France clinched the 1984 Grand Slam — has made an immense contribution to the game both on and off the field.

His legendary sense of humour has brought fun into a sport where sometimes it appears to be missing. When he captained Scotland for the first time against Wales in 1989, the difficult and strained post-match Press conference was turned into a Calder special. He arrived eating a Mars bar, sat down and told the waiting writers in classic soccer style: 'The boys done what was required of them over the 80 minutes . . . we are over the moon . . . definitely not sick as parrots. Anything else, lads?' Similarly on the Thursday before the Grand Slam decider, he and his colleagues set up a sublime practical joke on the hapless John Jeffrey while enjoying a pint in an Edinburgh pub. A young girl burst in, confronted Finlay and told him in a loud voice that her test was positive and what did he plan to do about it. Mock surprise and concern from the rest of the party and the genuine article from JJ as he tried to help his back-row pal out of a very sticky situation. Fin Calder recalls: 'You would not believe the look on JJ's face. We kept it going right through that night and only broke the news that it was a wind-up the following day on the way to training. It was superb.'

On a more serious note he tells of his decision not to play against Fiji last autumn which many saw as a snub which could have dented his international prospects. It did no such thing of course and he says: 'There is no way a man of my age could have trained for the Fiji game and kept a level of fitness up right through the season with a game like that one against England and a tour to New Zealand to follow. I have been working up to peak in New Zealand . . . We have got to remember we are not as young as we used to be. Look at Jeff Probyn and Paul Rendall. At 1 p.m. on Saturday they were the best props in the world; by 4 p.m. they looked just a couple of tired old jokers. That will never happen to me.'

He suggests that there was a gradual build-up of the Scottish performance over the season — about 60 per cent against Ireland, 70 per cent against France and 75 per cent against Wales. 'I always knew we had that extra quarter left to give and in the end it proved we had even more. If it is possible to give 110 per cent then that is what we gave. I don't think we can get better but we can be just as good if we take the pride and commitment shown at Murrayfield to New Zealand with us.'

Fin believes there will be great support for the tourists down under. 'There is a large Scots contingent and I believe the fans are getting bored with the Kiwis never meeting anyone who can give them a game. We will give them a game, that is for sure.'

He helped in the 'low key' approach to the final match by telling younger players how to deal with the media and just letting the English players start to believe they were invincible. 'I gave them a bit of chat at the tail of the lineout, just saying how welcome they were being world-beaters and all that. In the end we simply stitched them up.'

The rugby man in Fin Calder was never seen to better effect than when he consoled Brian Moore, the English hooker, as he sat head in hands close to tears of frustration. Brian Moore later paid public tribute to his Lions captain, doubting whether he could have done the same. Fin shrugged it off with the words: 'The man was absolutely shattered, I couldn't pass him by.'

DEREK WHITE: *No 8*
Full name: *Derek Bolton White*
Born: *30 January 1958, Dunbar*
Height: *6ft. 4in.*
Weight: *15st. 10lb.*
Caps: *24, first against France, 1982*
Clubs: *London Scottish, Gala*
Education: *Dunbar Grammar*
Occupation: *sales manager*
Married: *to Audrey, 'no family but two dogs which are hard enough work'*

Most of these great rugby players answered 'the final whistle against England' when asked for a great moment and Derek White was no exception. It took him no time at all, though, to come up with the second highlight — his second try against the Irish in Dublin. He recalls with great glee: 'Dunbar was called, the move named after my home town, which is quick channel one ball with me picking up and heading for the opposition stand-off, hopefully catching their back row on the hop. If I'm caught I turn and wait for the cavalry, usually in the form of JJ on the inside. I managed to hand off the flanker, O'Hara I think, and headed towards the line. I saw a gap appear and went for it, managing to get to the line and get the ball over at full stretch.'

He laughs when asked if his pace is always so electrifying over 30 yards and adds: 'I would never describe my pace as electrifying but it was just about enough on the day.'

His sad departure from the field with knee-ligament damage in the Calcutta Cup game led to a quick word with the doctor, an ice pack and the donning of a track suit to get back to the bench and watch the rest of the game. 'The leg hurt a bit but I still managed to leap what seemed like 20 feet into the air when the whistle blew.'

He is thoroughly enjoying his time with London Scottish but finds English rugby 'very different' despite his club's attempts to play it like they do north of the Border. 'They've got big heavy forwards and we have really got to keep the ball away from them in order to play our running game.'

Derek is delighted to have been able to change his mind about the New Zealand tour and is looking forward to a return to that country.

GARY ARMSTRONG: *scrum-half*
Full name: *Gary Armstrong*
Born: *30 September 1966, Edinburgh*
Height: *5ft. 10in.*
Weight: *13st.*
Caps: *11, first against Australia, 1988*
Club: *Jed-Forest*
Education: *Jedburgh Grammar, Dunfermline High School*
Occupation: *lorry driver*
Married: *to Shona*

If in the mind of anyone Gary Armstrong was ever in the shadow of his Jed-Forest club-mate and Scotland predecessor, Roy Laidlaw, then the young scrum-half has now fully emerged.

His contribution to the Lions' tour of Australia and then to the Grand Slam season was immense, never more so than against England when his work rate verged on the superhuman and his eclipse of Richard Hill was total.

He remains consistently self-effacing, however, and points to the team effort which made his job that bit easier. One may have been entitled to expect the name Laidlaw to emerge when Gary is asked about major influences on his rugby career but instead he replies without hesitation: 'My wife Shona and the rest of my family have been the biggest influence. They have given me tremendous support all the time and it is them I must thank for the success which has come my way.'

Like that team effort, the media hype, explored elsewhere in these pages, is a recurring theme with all the players and Armstrong describes his reaction to it thus: 'It all began to get on top of some of us a wee bit. It is not nice to be written off but with the help of the senior players we established a reaction to it which came out in Saturday's game. I have never felt so keyed up and never wanted to win a game more than that one.'

The fitness of the players was patently obvious and Gary praised the work being done on 'fitness methods' which were brought to Scotland partly by New Zealand-based Scot, Jim Blair. These have filtered through the Scottish squad and to Riverside Park through Roy Laidlaw who is a coaching adviser with the SRU. 'Roy has given me quite a few pointers over the years and has helped the club a lot since he retired. It is great for the club that we have both been involved with the Lions and with great Scottish teams. I am pleased with the way I have played but the credit does not go to me or any one player, it goes to the squad and the coaches.'

CRAIG CHALMERS: *stand-off*
Full name: *Craig Minto Chalmers*
Born: *15 October 1968, Galashiels*
Height: *5ft. 10in.*
Weight: *12st. 5lb.*
Caps: *nine, first against Wales, 1989*
Club: *Melrose*
Education: *Melrose Grammar School, Earlston High School*
Occupation: *marketing representative*
Married: *no*

With the impetuousness of youth, Craig Chalmers disarmingly chooses Melrose winning the Division One title as the highlight of his rugby season then adds quickly: 'Perhaps I think that because it came first and the Grand Slam decider was still to come.' The decisive game against Jed-Forest served to keep the minds of both Craig and Gary Armstrong, an opponent that day, off the momentous events of the following week which helped tremendously.

Craig rose sharply to fame; there were those who said it was far too early for this callow youth to pull on an international jersey and don the cap that goes with it. He quickly proved them all wrong, however, with his excellent tackling, powerful punting and incisive play-making and, of course, the part of his game which will stick in the mind when the Grand Slam 1990 is discussed.

Gavin Hastings was struggling with his kicking and the young man from Melrose was called up to take over. The effect was shattering. He recalls that first kick against England: 'I really thought it would go to Gavin as it was 40 metres out but David called me up and I was delighted to have a go.' That one went wide but Craig had set his sights and English indiscipline was duly punished on three occasions by the stand-off who appeared twice for Scotland B before his elevation to the senior ranks.

He shrugs it off as he has most things which have come his way in a glittering early rugby career: 'I do the kicking all the time for Melrose and I have been kicking pretty well so it was really no different at Murrayfield. Well, perhaps a little bit different as 50,000 people were there willing me to put the kicks over.'

Craig admits that the Lions tour was an immense thrill and that to return from that and have success in the Grand Slam was another milestone in his career. What is left? 'I still have a lot to learn and I am learning from great players and great coaches. Who knows what is to come but I am sure there are many good things waiting in the future.'

Of his kicks he admits, as Bill McLaren put it so graphically on television, they were a 'little bit inebriated' as they crossed the bar but Craig adds: 'They may not have been as sure as some of my other kicks at goal this season but they sure were as important.'

CRAIG CHALMERS

IWAN TUKALO: *wing*
Full name: *Iwan Tukalo*
Born: *5 March 1961, Edinburgh*
Height: *5ft. 9in.*
Weight: *12st. 9lb.*
Caps: *22, first against Ireland, 1985*
Club: *Selkirk*
Education: *Royal High School*
Occupation: *senior engineer*
Married: *to Susan with a 'distinct possibility of a family soon'*

Rather surprisingly, perhaps, Iwan Tukalo does not choose for a highlight any of his tries in the Grand Slam season — among the ten in his 22 internationals which began against Ireland not long after the last clean sweep for a Scotland side. Instead he cites the 'fabulous friendship' which has built up among the squad and which led to the kind of practical joke which Finlay Calder played on JJ not long before the Calcutta Cup encounter.

Of that, there is more elsewhere in these pages, but Iwan says: 'That is the kind of wind-up that only good mates can play on one another. These are good mates and great players, it has been a wonderful year. It was a fabulous atmosphere that Saturday and we all played above ourselves, after soaking up that atmosphere and being carried along with the crowd.'

He concedes that it is 'always nice to score tries' but adds that as 30 looms ever larger — age that is — the tries have to be worked for harder than ever before and he has to work harder to keep his fitness. 'I have, though, and long may it continue.'

The Selkirk winger admits that Scotland 'did not set the heather on fire' in the first few internationals and calls the victories which led to the Grand Slam decider 'workmanlike'. Yet he cites the away victories in Dublin and Cardiff — against opposition 'on the rebound' — as being the corner-stone of the Grand Slam victory. His only regret was not being 'quoted' for the Lions tour last summer but adds: 'When you finish a season with your country winning the lot and your club staying in the First Division it reminds you that you don't really have much to complain about.'

SEAN LINEEN: *centre*
Full name: *Sean Raymond Patrick Lineen*
Born: *25 December 1961, Auckland, New Zealand*
Height: *6ft. 1in.*
Weight: *13st. 9lb.*
Caps: *ten, first against Wales, 1989*
Club: *Boroughmuir*
Education: *Edgewater College, Auckland*
Occupation: *property manager*
Married: *no*

The singing of 'Flower of Scotland' shortly before half-past two on the Saturday that the Calcutta Cup and all the glittering prizes were competed for is undoubtedly the best moment for this adopted son of Scotland. He says unequivocally that these were the greatest few minutes of his life and adds: 'I had never felt anything like it in my life and if I do again I will be a very fortunate man.'

Without labouring the point it must be noted that the tall 'second five-eighths' from New Zealand rather surprisingly appeared on the international scene after arriving in the land of his grandfather — that gentleman was from Stornoway — and joining the far-thinking Boroughmuir club in Edinburgh where the selectors were happy to offer him a place in the team and the entrepreneurial Norrie Rowan was able to offer him gainful employment. He makes no bones about the fact that his was a right-place-at-the-right-time success story as both Edinburgh and Scotland were on the lookout for a centre of quality.

Sean fitted like a hand in a glove and has helped Scotland enormously in his own quiet way to their success. His partnership with Scott Hastings has been a success on the field and has spilled over into a personal friendship which has seen them become inseparable pals, living life to the full in Edinburgh and beyond.

The explosive tackling of both centre partners has been a feature of Scotland's successful defence but for Sean there is one regret. 'Scott and I have not been able to show our attacking qualities so much in the Grand Slam season as we would have liked. Because of the way the games have gone and the game plan, quite understandably, has meant that we have been doing the defending and not getting the ball in our hands as we love to do.'

Sean is hugely proud of what he has achieved and is sure that his pride is shared by father, Terry, who played 12 times for the All Blacks. 'What may be difficult for Dad and the rest of the family will be when we take on the All Blacks in the Test matches. I hope that he will be shouting for us despite his links with New Zealand. Whatever happens it will be a great honour and I am sure we will have a great time and enjoy some great rugby.'

SCOTT HASTINGS: *centre*
Full name: *Scott Hastings*
Born: *12 December 1964, Edinburgh*
Height: *6ft. 1in.*
Weight: *13st. 4lb.*
Caps: *23, first against France, 1986*
Club: *Watsonians*
Education: *George Watson's College, Newcastle Polytechnic*
Occupation: *advertising account executive*
Married: *no*

Scott Hastings is as firm in his appraisal of Scotland's performance this season as he is in his tackling. 'The best is yet to come; we were good but we can get better.' This is not an idle boast: like all the players he was delighted with the wins, but like Sean Lineen and perhaps the wingers, he would perhaps have liked to see, as he puts it, 'the flow come as we all know it can'.

But the centre who delighted Watsonians at home and abroad by remaining loyal to, and captaining, his old school's FP rugby side, despite their slide into the Second Divison and doubtless many offers to move to a Division One side, feels the potential is there. 'The line in international rugby between a move breaking down and a player making a telling break is so fine that you never know what might happen. On two or three occasions in all the matches there was a chink of light and we were called back for an infringement. It is very frustrating but you just have to get on with the job in hand.'

He dismisses his excellent tackling all season — his chopping of Rory Underwood at a vital stage in the game against England will live in the memory for a long time — as 'just doing the chores that I am there for' and adds with his winning smile: 'I think Gavin Hastings was lurking about behind me somewhere and I am sure he would have got him anyway before any damage was done.'

He feels that both the Lions tour and the Scotland trip to Japan, despite the squad being split up for these journeys, was 'particularly important' for the success of this past season and joins his colleagues in praising most highly one Ian McGeechan while not forgetting Messrs Telfer, Grant and Morgan.

TONY STANGER: *wing*
Full name: *Anthony George Stanger*
Born: *14 May 1968, Hawick*
Height: *6ft. 2in.*
Weight: *13st. 7lb.*
Caps: *six, first against Fiji, 1989*
Club: *Hawick*
Education: *Wilton Primary, Hawick High School*
Occupation: *bank officer*
Married: *no*

Young Tony Stanger, the 'wunderkind' of the Grand Slam squad, is in absolutely no doubt what his favourite moment of the season — and probably his rugby career so far — must be. 'When I felt the ball in my hands and dived over for the try against England I was absolutely thrilled,' he says.

The 21-year-old Hawick player has clearly switched on to the humour wavelength of his senior colleagues when he quips: 'It's maybe just as well it fell on my wing as who knows what would have happened if Iwan Tukalo at five feet nine had been going for the ball!' What is certain is that the player who has now scored six tries in as many internationals had to stretch to his full six foot two inches to secure the try which many see as having sealed Grand Slam success for Scotland.

This product of the famous Hawick High School now looks forward to the 'learning experience' of New Zealand then returning to club business as Hawick rebuild with their young team. 'I hope that a good centre comes along next season because, although I have not minded helping out, I see myself as a winger and want to learn as much as I can about the angles of running, tactics and so on in that position.'

TONY STANGER

GAVIN HASTINGS: *full-back*
Full name: *Andrew Gavin Hastings*
Born: *3 January 1962, Edinburgh*
Height: *6ft. 2in.*
Weight: *15st.*
Caps: *24, first against France, 1986*
Club: *London Scottish, Watsonians*
Education: *George Watson's College, Cambridge University*
Occupation: *agency surveyor*
Married: *no*

It was not difficult for this most sociable of rugby men to pick a favourite moment from his Grand Slam year. 'Waking up on the Sunday morning after the England game, reading every paper I could lay my hands on and then heading down for breakfast and a couple of quiet pints to see some of the lads and find out what they had been up to the night before,' he says.

His experience was invaluable throughout the championship but he attributes a large part of Scotland's success to the feeling of confidence and camaraderie which Scotland's Lions from the Australian tour brought back. 'We really felt we could do it and passed on that kind of confidence to the rest of the squad. Once you combine that sort of confidence with the work being put in by the best coaches in the world — Ian McGeechan and Jim Telfer — you have a powerful and ultimately winning combination.'

The tall and elegant full-back cites the crowd as another telling factor in the final leg of the race for the glittering prizes and asks: 'What chance did the English have playing against, ultimately, 16 Scots on the park and 50,000 around the stadium?'

The recurring theme of team-work raises itself again when Gavin is asked about his disappointing kicking form and the ultimate decision to leave the place-kicks to young Craig Chalmers. 'There was absolutely no problem with that. We all knew what we had to do, Craig was kicking well and I just went up to hold in the wind and give him every encouragement and all the support I could.'

Gavin admits to returning to earth very slowly after the weekend of 17 March but there is a feeling of satisfaction when he recalls the media hype surrounding the English camp and his team-mates' reaction to it. 'We were all getting a bit fed up with all the nonsense being written and spoken about what was and was not going to happen on Grand Slam Saturday. It was tempting to have a go back but this was resisted by the whole team until that final slow walk out of the tunnel with the noise washing over us. It was a call to arms; we responded to the crowd and they responded to us. At times it was as if they were down on the field beside us, willing us on to even greater effort.'

REPLACEMENTS

CRAIG REDPATH: *full-back/wing*
Full name: *Alexander Craig Redpath*
Born: *21 September 1969, Galashiels*
Height: *6ft.*
Weight: *13st.*
Caps: *none*
Club: *Melrose*
Education: *Kelso High School, Dundee Institute*
Occupation: *student of applied economics*
Married: *no*

The Melrose utility player thought that things could not get better in his rugby season. His team had secured the national league title, he was leading the South at under-21 level to what was ultimately to be the retention of their championship and was playing better than ever.

Then came the call from the Scottish Rugby Union — his services were required to cover for Gavin Hastings and be among the replacements on a day on which history would be made. He recalls: 'I was absolutely thrilled but at the same time sorry for Peter Dods because I knew I was being called in because he had suffered an unfortunate injury that Saturday in the leagues. The welcome I got from the rest of the guys was unbelievable and what made it even better was that Peter was there and saying he was delighted I had taken his place on the bench, giving me loads of support and encouragement.'

The young full-back-cum-centre — his versatility has led to a call-up for the Scotland tour to New Zealand — finds it hard to choose between the Melrose triumph and his international call-up for a season highlight but adds: 'Whatever happens I owe a lot to Jim Telfer who has taught me and so many other people so much about the game and how to prepare ourselves for the big matches. I am excited about the tour and will just have to wait and see how rugby is going to fit in with my studies and my future career. At the moment I am just having a great time playing rugby with some great people.'

CRAIG REDPATH

DOUGLAS WYLLIE: *stand-off/centre*
Full name: *Douglas Stewart Wyllie*
Born: *20 May 1963, Edinburgh*
Height: *6ft.*
Weight: *12st. 4lb.*
Caps: *ten, first against Australia, 1984*
Club: *Stewart's-Melville FP*
Education: *Daniel Stewart's and Melville College*
Occupation: *sales representative*
Married: *to Jennifer*

Dougie Wyllie became, quite understandably, a bit fed up when all the Grand Slam stories identified Peter Dods as the only link between the triumphs of 1984 and 1990. It is a pleasure to set the record straight — Douglas Stewart Wyllie was on the bench throughout that season's Five Nations' Championship and, indeed, won his first cap that year against Australia.

This effective utility player cannot quite remember the spread of his ten caps — he thinks that six of them have been at stand-off and four at centre. He says: 'Like my fellow replacements there can be moments of frustration at not being on the field, but this is the kind of squad where everyone has a part to play in the ultimate success. We train to as high a level, we must know every move backwards and be ready, as Derek Turnbull discovered, to go on at a moment's notice.' Dougie's reaction to being described as one of the senior players is mock outrage. 'Wait a minute, I'm only 26.' Then he concedes that from 1983, when he first moved into the reckoning with a seat on the bench as the 25-25 draw with the All Blacks was fought out, until now is quite a long time and it is fair to think of him being on the scene 'forever'. The last half-hour of the Calcutta Cup was watched from a standing position by most of the stand-by squad, as Dougie explains: 'Normally we do a bit of shouting from the bench, me more than most, but show a bit of decorum. This time all caution was thrown to the winds and we were on our feet shouting the boys on. It was a wonderful experience and if it means sitting on the bench to be part of it, then so be it.'

DOUGLAS WYLLIE

177

GREIG OLIVER: *scrum-half*
Full name: *Greig Hunter Oliver*
Born: *12 September 1964, Hawick*
Height: *5ft. 8½in.*
Weight: *12st. 6lb.*
Caps: *one, against Zimbabwe in the World Cup, 1987*
Club: *Hawick*
Education: *Hawick High School, Napier College*
Occupation: *newspaper compositor*
Married: *no*

The attitude of this young man, who has been the 'eternal bridesmaid' of Scottish international rugby, perhaps epitomises more than anything what it means to be part of the top flight. Greig Oliver has sat on the bench no fewer than 22 times for Scotland, understudying Roy Laidlaw for two seasons and now standing by as lieutenant to Gary Armstrong. His solitary cap came against Zimbabwe in the 1987 World Cup. Yet there is not a hint of bitterness and only a smidgen of frustration when he says: 'It is fantastic to be involved in the set-up and no player could complain at being considered next best to guys of the quality of Roy and Gary. This has been a disappointing season at club level as Hawick are rebuilding a young side but at international level it has been fantastic.'

Greig is excited about the prospect of returning to New Zealand where he won that first cap. 'It's a wonderful place to play rugby. The whole country is steeped in it and you walk down the street and meet an old lady who starts chatting and knows more about rugby than you do.'

The man whose prolific left boot, they say, will be encased in gold and kept in the Hawick club-rooms when it is hung up with its neighbour, is pleased with his personal performance this season and says that more than anything the 'down-to-earth attitude' in the Borders particularly, and Scotland generally, has helped him and his colleagues. 'You never get above yourself with Jim Telfer or Terence Froud (Hawick coach) around and that, in a way, is what happened to some of those English fellows who were coming up to claim their Grand Slam as a matter of course. It didn't quite work out that way, did it?'

DEREK TURNBULL: *flanker*
Full name: *Derek James Turnbull*
Born: *2 October 1961, Hawick*
Height: *6ft. 4in.*
Weight: *15st. 5lb.*
Caps: *four, first against New Zealand in the World Cup, 1987*
Club: *Hawick*
Education: *Hawick High School*
Occupation: *police officer*
Married: *due to marry in August*

The big Hawick policeman characteristically expresses regret that Derek White had to be hurt to allow him his fourth cap, then elation as the memory of being called on as replacement drifts back. 'I saw Derek going down while I was still on the bench and he seemed to be improving. I was told to go down to the tunnel and start warming up. I kept thinking this was the fourth or fifth time in my career I had been warming up with my track suit off, only to be told it was a false alarm. Then came the call, Derek limped past but took time to say good luck and issue a few pointers. It was some feeling running on to the park with that noise all around.'

Derek Turnbull is one of many players who describes the atmosphere in the Scotland squad as akin to that of a club side. He adds: 'There is a great, close friendship among the boys and we are lucky enough to meet each other on club Saturdays, at district championship time and of course at squad sessions. That kind of spirit is shown nowhere better than on the field of play.'

ALEX BREWSTER: *prop*
Full name: *Alexander Kinloch Brewster*
Born: *3 May 1954, Edinburgh*
Height: *6ft.*
Weight: *15st. 2lb.*
Caps: *six, first against England, 1977*
Club: *Stewart's-Melville FP*
Education: *Melville College, Edinburgh University*
Occupation: *farmer*
Married: *to Pamela, with six-year-old son, Scott, and daughters, Jane, four, Michelle, two and one-year-old Caroline*

There are myriad special memories for the evergreen utility forward from Stewart's-Melville FP. After a few moments' thought he says: 'I would have to say that the whole season has been one long highlight.'

This most loyal and hard-working of Scotland's rugby servants has been honoured with caps six times. Yet the more astonishing statistic concerning the man who will be 36 by the time Scotland travel down under is that he has been involved in squad sessions for 14 years. However, he speaks with some regret of his switch from 'genuine open-side flanker' into the front row midway through his international career. 'I had a major operation on knee ligaments and this took a few yards off my pace. I switched to prop, continued to play for the district and was fortunate enough to remain in the international reckoning,' he recalls.

Alex still has the same hunger for the game and the same joy at being involved with the squad and touring as he did in 1989, captaining the Scotland party in Japan. He says: 'I have a large family and a large farm which occupy my mind all year round. It is great to get away on tour and concentrate on nothing but rugby for a few weeks.' Of his international career he says: 'I have had great fun for 14 years with various squads and I am here to be involved as long as I am required.'

JOHN ALLAN: *hooker*
Full name: *John Allan*
Born: *25 November 1963, Glasgow*
Height: *6ft.*
Weight: *14st. 7lb.*
Caps: *none*
Club: *Edinburgh Academicals*
Education: *Craigend Primary, Sella Wood and Glenwood High Schools,*
           Durban Technicon, South Africa
Occupation: *property manager*
Married: *no*

The rise of John Allan from interesting newcomer to international prospect probably surprised the quiet Scot who had spent most of his 26 years in South Africa most of all. It gave him immense pride but, it must be said, his appointment put a few noses out of joint among those who felt that they were the heirs-apparent to the Scotland hooking berth.

What seemed to catch the eye was Allan's scrummaging power and all-round fitness and speed, which suited the Scotland game-plan. The powerful player, whom no less a person than his employer and former international prop, Norrie Rowan, describes as 'the best scrummaging hooker I have packed down with', began his career as a full-back but converted to hooker at the age of 15 and played for South African schools at rugby and softball. He was on the bench for the famous Natal provincial team before joining the Scottish team in 1989 and, playing 22 times before the lure of Scotland became overwhelming, he headed to his spiritual home where, with good friend and fellow exile, Sean Lineen, he moved swiftly into the international reckoning.

PETER DODS: *full-back/wing*
Full name: *Peter William Dods*
Born: *6 January 1958, Galashiels*
Height: *5ft. 8in.*
Weight: *11st. 10lb.*
Caps: *19, first against Ireland, 1983*
Club: *Gala*
Education: *Galashiels Academy*
Occupation: *sales representative*
Married: *to Hazel, with two daughters Lindsay, aged five, and two-year-old Lucy*

Perhaps in the best tradition of these things the best story is being left until last. Peter Dods, at 32, is one of only two direct links between Scotland's Grand Slam victories in 1984 and 1990. He was the full-back throughout that wonderful year and, despite being displaced by Gavin Hastings for three seasons, he was never far away from the international scene — returning to his berth last season as replacement when the senior Hastings was injured.

The quiet man refuses to compare the two Grand Slam sides as 'the teams and the circumstances were so unlike each other' but admits that his joy was just the same to be involved in the 1990 squad as it had been six years before.

Having 'picked up a knock' in the league game against Heriot's a week before the Calcutta Cup game, diagnosed as a depressed cheekbone fracture, he lost his chance to sit on the bench. The mental depression, if not the physical one, was quickly lifted, though, when he was assured that he would be part of the squad even if he were to be in a blazer and flannels instead of a track suit. 'That was a great feeling, remaining part of the squad. I was with the boys throughout the day and sat with them during the game, sharing their excitement right through to the final whistle and beyond to the wonderful celebrations after the match. That was one dinner I would not have wished to miss and I was so glad that I did not have to,' he says.

The record of the Gala full-back is remarkable. He has toured with either Scotland or the British Lions every year since 1980 and will again travel to New Zealand in May with the squad. He holds the district appearance record, having turned out 78 times for the South and has scored 646 points — almost double that of his nearest challenger, Andy Irvine from Edinburgh.

Dods says of the Grand Slam success: 'We brought back a tremendous amount of knowledge and confidence from the Lions tour and that showed through as the season progressed. It was a great squad to be involved with and I look forward to being involved for a while yet.'

EPILOGUE

FLOWER POWER

Much More Than a Song

By DEREK DOUGLAS

AND FINALLY, the part played in the Scottish victory by the SRU's decision to permit the pre-match singing of a Scottish anthem cannot be overstressed. But what an anthem. And at Murrayfield on Calcutta Cup day, 'Flower of Scotland', that wonderful evocation of Scottish martial prowess against the Auld Enemy, was quite simply the right song in the right place at the right time.

David Sole, dark and brooding, had just led his men out on to the pitch with that chilling gladiatorial tread. The English had pranced out moments before looking like leggy yearlings. The two teams lined up in front of the West stand for the usual rendering of 'God Save the Queen'. Then, after a momentary pause, the pipes and drums of the Queen Victoria School, Dunblane, struck up the first chords of 'Flower of Scotland'.

The effect was electrifying. Fifty thousand Scots voices took up the refrain:

> *O Flower of Scotland*
> *When will we see your like again*
> *That fought and died for*
> *Your wee bit hill and glen*
> *And stood against him*
> *Proud Edward's army*
> *And sent him homeward*
> *Tae think again*

Then, for the first time, the Murrayfield crowd, with the words printed in the programme, launched into a second verse with an intensity and a gusto that made the hairs stand up on the back of the neck.

189

Those days are passed now
And in the past they must remain
But we can still rise now
And be the nation again
That stood against him
Proud Edward's army
And sent him homeward
Tae think again *

By now, as the wave of sound swirled around the packed stadium, the crowd in far-flung parts of the ground were out of synchronisation. But no matter, the intensity of feeling was overwhelming.

Throughout this amazing performance, the likes of which had never been witnessed before, the England team, looking uneasy in the extreme, were forced to stand, look, and, above all, listen to the passionate defiance of the nation they had come to vanquish. Truly the emotion and the theatre of the occasion was worth three points to the Scottish team before even a ball had been kicked.

Among the crowd, seated in the West stand with his daughter, Lauren, was one half of The Corries singing duo, Ronnie Browne. Poignantly, the author of the song, the other Corrie, Roy Williamson, was not there. He was at home recovering from a brain tumour and had been undergoing radiotherapy. Says Browne, who used to turn out for the Boroughmuir Club in Edinburgh: 'It was absolutely incredible. The emotion was overwhelming. I just couldn't get the first line out. I just choked and it took me a while to recover. I have never heard a Scottish crowd singing like that before and to be in the middle of it all was the most amazingly emotional experience.

'The song was particularly appropriate for that day. It's about the Auld Enemy. It was directed at them and I could see the effect it was having on the English team. It was quite, quite magnificent.'

But the song has also received the Royal stamp of approval. Princess Anne, the Princess Royal, patron of the Scottish Rugby Union, was present at the match with son, Peter, and daughter, Zara. A few days later the Princess was taking part in an official visit to Warminster, Wiltshire. With the stirring tones of 50,000 Scots still ringing in her ears the Princess told Scots-born Citizens' Advice Bureau worker, Grace Curtis, that the song had galvanised the Scottish players into action. 'I'm surprised English sports teams don't sing "Land of Hope and Glory",' said the Princess.

Ronnie Browne's involvement with the match has not ended with the song. He produced the official painting of Scotland's 1984 Grand Slam, *The Turning Point*, which depicts Jim Calder's try. He has been commissioned by the Royal Bank to complete a unique double and produce a similar memento to commemorate the 1990 triumph as well.

And wasn't he right about that afternoon at Murrayfield? It was indeed, quite, quite, magnificent.

* © The Corries (Music) Ltd
Printed by kind permission of The Corries